Small

Business

Start-up & Growth

Guide for Beginners

Thank you so much for purchasing this book and allowing me to guide you on your small business journey.

As an independent author, reviews are incredibly helpful in reaching new readers and getting this important information to other small business owners. If you enjoyed the book and have a moment, I would be so grateful if you would consider leaving a review on Amazon or wherever you purchased the book. Your honest feedback makes a huge difference.

If you'd like to connect for other resources and updates that will help you grow your small business, please follow the QR code below.

Thanks again for your support!

Table of Contents

"The most difficult thing is the decision to act, the rest is merely tenacity."
- Amelia Earhart

Introduction

Welcome to the World of Small Business!

Congratulations on deciding to take the first step in creating your own business and taking control of your destiny. Whether you decided to take this first step because of a job loss, or this is a dream you've had for many years and you just didn't have the time or courage to make it a reality, I applaud your decision. Millions of individuals share your dream of entrepreneurship, but few take steps to make it happen and even fewer have the tools they need to be successful.

I created this guide for a couple of reasons. First, because I work with small business owners in my CPA firm on a daily basis and watch the struggles they have in knowing where to start. Understanding LLCs vs sole proprietorships vs S-Corporations, wrapping their heads around the insanely complicated tax system, and most importantly, tracking their finances to allow them to make timely and accurate decisions within their business can be overwhelming. Bookkeeping is a task most business owners dread. But if there is one thing that many business owners learn the hard way, it is that you cannot pivot quickly to take advantage of new opportunities, or avoid potentially disastrous pitfalls, if you don't know your numbers.

Second, I have been in your shoes. Whether you've been too anxious to follow your dream, or you're picking up this book out of a necessity to provide for your family, I can empathize from first-hand experience. I spent fifteen years working for others and growing their firms, all while secretly dreaming of setting out on my own and creating a practice that followed my vision. I didn't have the confidence to take that first step as it was a huge financial risk and I had a family that depended on my salary.

A firm merger and the roller coaster that followed eventually provided me with the push I needed to take the leap and venture out on my own. It was a whirlwind of changes and my head was swimming with all the tasks required to create a new business. The prospect was overwhelming and scary and I felt like I was drowning at times. I had the background and experience to tackle this task, but there were times imposter syndrome kicked in and I doubted my decision.

Amidst the chaos, I took a deep breath and quickly realized I knew where to begin. I just had to cut through the doubt and insecurities. I had walked thousands of business owners through creating, growing, and winding down their entities. I also had training as a CPA and business coach which gave me the resources I needed to take action and make quick decisions. Without missing a beat, I was meeting with clients in my new office and under a new LLC. All within just a few days of leaving my old firm. It was the craziest few days of my life, but years later I can also tell you it was the absolute best decision of my career. An unexpected situation became a blessing in disguise.

I want to walk you through the steps I took to create the true business of my dreams. A business that allows me to work how, when, and where I want, even in a world that is typically driven by deadlines and motivated by stress. I no longer work 7 days a week and I control the money I make. I will guide you through creating an entity that reflects you and not those that came before you. Your business will only succeed if you have a clear vision, actionable steps to follow, and a belief in yourself and what you bring to the table.

The Path of a Small Business

Whether you are in a situation that requires you to digest and utilize this guide in a weekend, or whether you slow-walk your business creation (the better method, to be honest), I want to give you a warm welcome. And I want to thank you for trusting me to guide you through this process. Your business will become like another family member and I hope it is a family member you are proud to nourish and grow over the years.

Chapter One

Saving Your Sanity by Setting Boundaries

A growing business needs systems and boundaries, or it can take over your life and become something you never anticipated. Note initial boundaries for yourself and your customers. When you're tempted to step into forbidden territory, ask yourself whether this will further your business goals or whether it's a knee-jerk reaction to an outside stressor. Pull yourself back from any decisions or projects that don't ultimately grow your business and provide the work/life balance you are working to achieve.

Project and/or Client Boundaries

Preferred Projects & Clients	Out of Bounds Projects & Clients

How firm are these boundaries? When will you make exceptions?

_____

_____

_____

_____

_____

_____

_____

_____

_____

_____

Time Boundaries

Hours Available to Clients or In Shop	Days & Hours Off the Clock

How firm are these boundaries? When will you make exceptions?

_____

_____

_____

_____

_____

_____

_____

_____

_____

_____

Financial Boundaries

Amount Willing to Invest in Business	Limits on Financial Contributions

How firm are these boundaries? When will you make exceptions?

_____

_____

_____

_____

_____

_____

_____

_____

_____

_____

Chapter Two

Designing the Business YOU Want

Launching a new business brings an abundance of emotions. Excitement. Fear. Stress. Doubt. Overwhelm. These are all perfectly normal and you are not alone in these feelings. All new entrepreneurs have been there, and seasoned entrepreneurs still feel these when big changes happen.

Much like bringing a new baby or puppy into your life, there are joys to embrace, but also stumbling blocks you didn't see coming. You will pour your blood, sweat, and tears into this business as it grows. It will become a part of you and your family, and the journey can be an emotional and financial roller coaster at times.

However, there is a short exercise you can do to remove the overwhelm, clear the clutter from your mind, and create a path to a more streamlined and profitable business.

I performed this exercise as part of a mastermind group. I put my finished notes on a posterboard and hung it in my office. I still refer back to these ideas and basic framework when planning projects, social media posts, newsletter submissions, and client communications. It keeps me from getting lost in ideas that won't ultimately grow my business or bring value to my clients. You can never buy more time, so why waste it on implementing ideas that don't fit your ultimate goals?

The Sticky Note Exercise

For this exercise, I highly recommend hiding in a quiet space for an hour so you can fully focus on getting your ideas down on paper. Don't labor over this project for too long as it's simply meant to get the clutter out of your head and down on paper.

We'll use the rough framework created here to build the shell of your business throughout the remaining chapters of this book.

What you'll need:

- Different colored sticky notes
- Marker
- Posterboard (to save final notes you can refer back to later and tweak as your business grows)

Create sticky notes with 6 main headings. I used a different color for each to help differentiate the parts of the business I was focusing on.

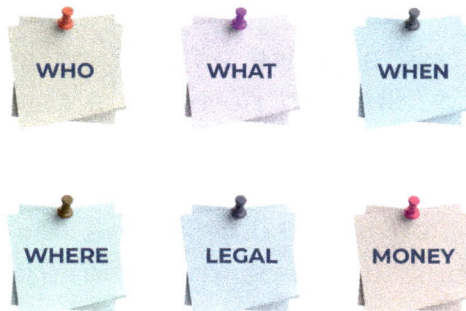

WHO   WHAT   WHEN

WHERE   LEGAL   MONEY

Spend the next hour quickly jotting down ideas or tasks under each of the main headings. Put each on a separate sticky note so you can scrap ideas that don't make sense later. The goal is to declutter the process and focus only on the most meaningful ideas or tasks.

For example, when focusing on "Where" & "When", you may have:

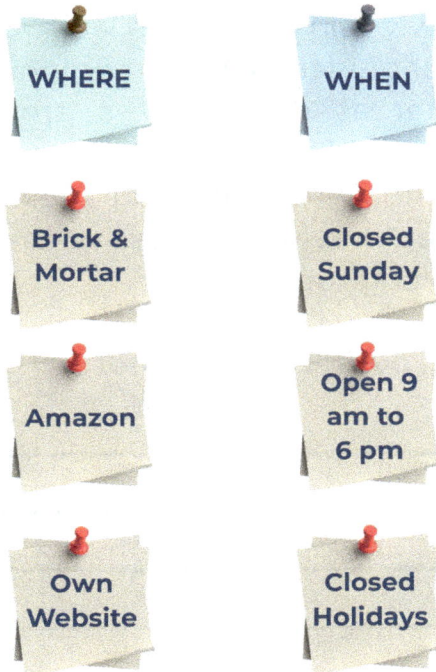

WHERE	WHEN
Brick & Mortar	Closed Sunday
Amazon	Open 9 am to 6 pm
Own Website	Closed Holidays

Don't get lost in the weeds. Later chapters will guide you through the putting the pieces of the puzzle together. And your business will morph and grow over the following months and years. Don't feel like you have to have all the answers today. Focus on the basics and then pivot as your personal needs and customer wants drive the business forward.

Who - Who will you offer your product or service to? Be very specific about your intended client or customer. Focus on demographics such as age, hobbies, income level, spending habits, and pain points they may be feeling. If you are selling a premier product, you won't want to target your advertising to customers on a tight budget.

Also make note of any professionals you will need to hire. Many new business owners later regret skimping on professional guidance in the beginning. Employees can come later as the business grows. But hiring professionals to aid in setting up your legal entity, handling your finances, or getting a marketing plan off the ground could result in massive time and money savings in the long run.

Age range of your ideal customer

_____

_____

_____

_____

_____

_____

_____

_____

_____

Hobbies, reading interests, weekend activities, and favorite shops of ideal customer

_____

_____

_____

_____

_____

_____

_____

_____

_____

Pain points ideal customer is trying to solve

_____

_____

_____

_____

_____

_____

_____

_____

_____

Benefits to flying solo during start-up phase

_____

_____

_____

_____

_____

_____

_____

_____

Contractors needed to help with specific projects

_____

_____

_____

_____

_____

_____

_____

_____

_____

Necessary employees and average pay in your area

_____

_____

_____

_____

_____

_____

_____

_____

_____

Partners involved & responsibilities/skill sets of each

_____

_____

_____

_____

_____

_____

_____

_____

_____

What - What product or service will you offer? Focus on your skill set, past experiences, and passions. Keeping in mind that you can't offer all things to all people, which of the products or services that appeal to you will also be marketable to your target audience? If you are opening a pizza place, but live in an area frequented by healthy eaters, a meat lover's option may not be your best seller, so don't spend time and money perfecting that pie.

You WILL be tempted to try a million different things when reaching for that first sale. Don't give in to that temptation. Remember your core customer and products and work on your message to reach that customer instead. Time and money are both precious. And you can never get back more time. Protect it by focusing your energies on your ultimate goal.

Your strengths & weaknesses

_____

_____

_____

_____

_____

_____

_____

_____

_____

_____

Services or products you would enjoy creating or providing to customers

_____

_____

_____

_____

_____

_____

_____

_____

_____

_____

Products or services to avoid offering

_____

_____

_____

_____

_____

_____

_____

_____

_____

Supplemental products or services (possible upsells)

_____

_____

_____

_____

_____

_____

_____

_____

_____

_____

Price points - budget conscious buyers or upscale purchasers?

_____

_____

_____

_____

_____

_____

_____

_____

_____

_____

Products or services that set you apart from the competition

_____

_____

_____

_____

_____

_____

_____

_____

_____

_____

When - What hours will you be available? Will you have set hours each day or week? If you are creating a service-based business, will you need an online calendar to schedule client appointments? Does your schedule need to be flexible to allow for family needs or a busy travel schedule? If your business is seasonal, how will your hours vary with changing business or client needs?

Days you will be open to the public

_____

_____

_____

_____

_____

_____

_____

_____

_____

Hours you will be available or will need to be off the clock

_____

_____

_____

_____

_____

_____

_____

_____

_____

Holidays or other special days you will not be available

_____

_____

_____

_____

_____

_____

_____

_____

_____

_____

Special events to consider (high sales volume/ additional help needed)

_____

_____

_____

_____

_____

_____

_____

_____

_____

_____

Family needs to consider in setting hours or closures

_____

_____

_____

_____

_____

_____

_____

_____

_____

Where- Where will you provide these services? Can you start off working from home? Is working virtually more your cup of tea? Do you need a virtual storefront or brick and mortar building? Start off as simply and inexpensively as possible. If you don't need a brick and mortar, don't be tempted to rent the biggest, fanciest space in town. The money you're spending on rent may be better spent on supplies, advertising, or investing in software. Finding and renovating a physical space can be an expensive and drawn-out process as well. Time and money is precious. Spend both as cautiously as possible when starting out.

If you will be fully virtual, I strongly encourage you to set up separate email addresses and phone numbers for the business. It can be convenient to let friends, family, and new customers use your cell phone in the beginning, but many come to regret this. Create ways that you can turn off the office after hours or when you're on vacation.

Home office or work space needed

_____

_____

_____

_____

_____

_____

_____

_____

_____

Necessity for brick and mortar space

_____

_____

_____

_____

_____

_____

_____

_____

_____

Online sales platforms to utilize (Etsy, Amazon, own website, etc)

_____

_____

_____

_____

_____

_____

_____

_____

_____

_____

In-person opportunities (craft shows, community events, etc)

_____

_____

_____

_____

_____

_____

_____

_____

_____

_____

3rd party retail options (offer commissions or wholesale pricing)

_____

_____

_____

_____

_____

_____

_____

_____

_____

Advertising platforms that will reach your ideal customer

_____

_____

_____

_____

_____

_____

_____

_____

_____

Legal - What will you name your business? Do you need a domain and customized email address? What legal form will your new business take? Will you need to create an LLC? Is starting off as a sole proprietor a better option? Are you creating a partnership with another individual? Don't worry if you don't know these answers yet. I will provide some basics in a later chapter where you can fill in the blanks.

This is also an area where you should focus some financial resources on professional legal guidance to protect your business and personal assets. An attorney can walk you through the logistics of creating an LLC in your state, the pros and cons of various options, and how to create an LLC that will actually protect you should an unfortunate legal situation arise.

Will you need to set up an LLC?

_____

_____

_____

_____

_____

_____

_____

_____

_____

If you are incorporating, which state will you incorporate in?

_____

_____

_____

_____

_____

_____

_____

_____

Will there be other partners and a need for a partnership agreement?

_____

_____

_____

_____

_____

_____

_____

_____

Do you need assistance purchasing property (such as land or a building)?

_____

_____

_____

_____

_____

_____

_____

_____

_____

Are you looking to trademark a name or other asset?

_____

_____

_____

_____

_____

_____

_____

_____

_____

Finances - What bank accounts will you need to set up? Don't be tempted to use your personal bank account. You should always separate your finances for both legal and financial purposes. How will you accept customer payments (Stripe, Square, etc)? What software will you use to track your income and spending? (It's ok to start out with a simple spreadsheet. Just use SOMETHING.) This is another important focus area. You cannot grow a business or be profitable if you don't know your numbers. You may also find that hiring a CPA or other professional will pay for itself in both cost and tax savings each year.

How many bank accounts will you need to set up (checking, savings, payroll, etc)?

_____

_____

_____

_____

_____

_____

_____

_____

_____

_____

Will you need to track inventory?

_____

_____

_____

_____

_____

_____

_____

_____

_____

_____

Will you need to run payroll or process invoices?

_____

_____

_____

_____

_____

_____

_____

_____

_____

_____

Will you need assistance setting up an accounting system? Will you use a spreadsheet or online system?

_____

_____

_____

_____

_____

_____

_____

_____

_____

Do you have the budget to hire someone to assist with your bookkeeping and tax planning/preparation?

_____

_____

_____

_____

_____

_____

_____

_____

_____

_____

_____

Will you need initial funding or investors to get your business off the ground?

_____

_____

_____

_____

_____

_____

_____

_____

_____

Will you need to use an online payment processor (such as Stripe or Square) to process customer payments?

_____

_____

_____

_____

_____

_____

_____

_____

_____

Why - Another important topic to address before creating your business is WHY you wanted to begin this journey. It could be as simple but important as saving money for a family vacation, or being able to spend more time with your children. Give this topic some very careful consideration and make an agreement with yourself now that you'll keep this reasoning in mind when making big business decisions. It's easy to get derailed when juggling multiple tasks and you may find that you're spending less time with your children instead of more. That's when you need to step back and rework things within the business to get it back on track.

_____

_____

_____

_____

_____

_____

_____

_____

_____

_____

Summarizing Your Ideas

Take the notes thoughts you've put down on paper in the previous sections and use those to create the initial vision of your business. Keep this information on hand when you start a new marketing plan, brainstorm a new product, or pivot on availability. It will help remind you of the market you're trying to reach and why you are on this journey in the first place.

WHO is your ideal customer/client?

_____

_____

_____

_____

_____

_____

_____

_____

WHAT will be your initial products/services?

_____

_____

_____

_____

_____

_____

_____

_____

_____

WHEN will you provide these products/services?

_____

_____

_____

_____

_____

_____

_____

_____

_____

WHERE will your business be located?

_____

_____

_____

_____

_____

_____

_____

_____

_____

What LEGAL formation is best? Have you hired an attorney?

_____

_____

_____

_____

_____

_____

_____

_____

_____

What are the initial FINANCIAL needs of your business?

_____

_____

_____

_____

_____

_____

_____

_____

_____

_____

"Those who let things happen usually lose to those who make things happen."
- Dave Weinbaum

Chapter Three

Creating Your Business Step-by-Step

Now that you've mapped out your vision, it's time to start taking steps to make this a reality. Since the goal of this guide is to get you up and running as quickly as possible in a limited amount of time, we'll focus on the basics. The following steps will lay a firm foundation which will allow your business to grow as quickly and profitably as possible.

Keep in mind that bigger isn't always better. Always remember that this is **your** dream and should fit **your** goals and financial aspirations. I personally downsized with my firm and changed my client focus after growing like crazy for three solid years. It was the best emotional and financial decision I ever made. I was too busy creating a business that mimicked firms I had worked for in the past. But those firm setups didn't work for me and my family. And I wanted to reach a different client base. Downsizing allowed me to better service clients, make more money and free up time for other pursuits.

▶ Determine Your Business Name

I'm sure you already have some ideas for your business name, but you'll want to ensure that you have the legal rights to use it and that any needed domain names and/or social media handles are available for marketing purposes. There's nothing worse than creating a website, ordering marketing materials, and creating a social media page, only to find out that you have to change your business name because someone else had the rights to it.

1. Come up with several business names that appeal to you.
2. Search your state business registry (Secretary of State) to determine which of the name(s) are available. (Most states require that business names be unique within the state you're registering.)
3. Check the US Patent and Trademark Office (USPTO) to determine if there are any trademarks on your chosen name.
4. Check domain registrars such as GoDaddy.com or Namecheap.com to determine if free domains are available to match your business name.
5. Search your favorite social media sites to determine if your preferred business handle is available.

Business Name - Option #1

_____

☐   Is the name available on your state registry?

☐   Is your initial trademark search clear of obvious issues?

Available domain(s)

_____

_____

_____

Available social media handle(s)

_____

_____

_____

Notes

_____

_____

_____

_____

_____

_____

_____

Business Name - Option #2

_____

☐   Is the name available on your state registry?

☐   Is your initial trademark search clear of obvious issues?

Available domain(s)

_____

_____

_____

Available social media handle(s)

_____

_____

_____

Notes

_____

_____

_____

_____

_____

_____

Business Name - Option #3

_____

☐ Is the name available on your state registry?

☐ Is your initial trademark search clear of obvious issues?

Available domain(s)

_____

_____

_____

Available social media handle(s)

_____

_____

_____

Notes

_____

_____

_____

_____

_____

_____

_____

Final Business Name Choice

_____

Domain Name

_____

Social Media Handle(s)

      Facebook _____

      Instagram _____

      TikTok   _____

      X   _____

2 ▶ Sole Proprietor or LLC

The next big step in your business creation is to determine whether you're going to operate as a sole proprietor *(or general partnership if there is more than one owner)* or if you would like to create legal liability protection for your business by creating a Legal Liability Company (LLC).

Sole Proprietor - A sole proprietorship is the simplest business structure. In most states you don't need to formally register to operate as a sole proprietor. All of your income is reported under your name and SSN. You may decide to create a "dba" ("doing business as") with your state for marketing purposes, but the IRS will still utilize your name and SSN for tax purposes. If you choose to operate as a sole proprietor, you simply need to start selling and report all of your income and expenses on a Schedule C. on your tax return.

The drawback to operating in this manner is that there is no legal separation between you and your business. This means that you could be held legally liable for any lawsuits against your business and both your business and personal assets could be at risk.

Legal Liability Company (LLC) - An LLC is a legal setup where your business is treated as its own entity—separate from you personally—but without all the complicated corporate hoops to jump through. It's like putting a shield around your personal assets (house, savings, your new car) so if the business hits a rough patch (lawsuits, debts), your personal assets usually stay safe. You can run it solo, with a partner, or even a group. Your personal finances are protected from business debts or legal trouble, as long as you don't mix things up (e.g., paying your mortgage with business cash).

Keep in mind whether you have legal liability concerns when deciding whether to go the route of a sole proprietor or whether you should enlist the aid of an attorney to create an LLC. Will you have a rental property where tenants could be injured? Are you selling food or other goods that could potentially cause harm to customers? Are you giving advice to clients that could be misunderstood and lead to financial losses?

Whether you intend to become an S-Corporation at

some point can also factor into this decision. You need to be incorporated before electing S-Corporation status with the IRS. Forming an LLC now can save you work down the road should electing to be an S-Corporation for tax purposes make sense.

▶ 3 Creating Your LLC

Should you decide that an LLC is the best legal structure for your business, services such as LegalZoom make setting up an LLC online fast and inexpensive. *However, I caution against performing this task without the assistance of an attorney.* LegalZoom, and other similar sites, generally warn that they are not providing legal advice. They are simply providing a software platform to make filing the necessary paperwork as simple as possible. And you may be able to file this same paperwork directly on your state's website without the added third-party filing fees. (State filing fees may still apply.)

Be sure to create an operating agreement. An LLC Operating Agreement is like the rulebook for your Limited Liability Company. It's not always required by law, but it's a smart move to keep your LLC's limited liability protection intact and your business running smoothly.

What to Include in an Operating Agreement:

- **Basic Info** - The LLC name, its purpose, and the state where it's formed

- **Ownership Detail** - List all members (owners) and their ownership percentages (e.g., you at 100% if solo, or you at 60%, your partner at 40%).
- **Management Structure** - Say if it's "member-managed" (you run it) or "manager-managed" (someone else does). Most solo LLCs are member-managed.
- **Profit and Loss Split** - Spell out how profits (and losses) are divided. This usually matches ownership splits (e.g., 100% to you if solo, or 50/50 if partnered and things are split evenly).
- **Contributions & Capital** - Note what each member contributed to start (e.g., "$100 cash," "a laptop worth $500"). Add rules for future contributions, if needed.
- **Decision-Making** - Define how big decisions happen (e.g., unanimous vote, majority rules). For solo, it's just "I decide".
- **Adding or Losing Members** - Detail rules for bringing in new members (e.g., "unanimous vote") or what happens if someone leaves (e.g., buyout terms & possible non-solicit rules)
- **Dissolution** - How the LLC ends (e.g., "if I quit or it goes bust, pay debts, split leftovers")
- **Books & Records** - Promise to track income, expenses, and decisions (e.g., "I'll keep a spreadsheet and receipts")
- **Signatures** - All members sign and date it (just you if solo)

Keep in mind that an LLC is only as good as your operating agreement and the steps you take to keep your business and personal activity separate. Laws regulating LLCs vary by state and you don't want to inadvertently pierce the corporate veil by commingling business and personal assets. You may take all the necessary steps to create your LLC, only to find that you inadvertently blew up all of your legal protections.

Here are some simple ways to protect your LLC:

- Keep business and personal finances separate
- File your LLC documents properly with the state and keep current with any annual filing fees
- Apply for an EIN, even if you don't need it
- Sign legal documents as the LLC, not as yourself
- Follow your operating agreement (even if you're running solo)
- Pay your taxes on time
- Get liability insurance
- Don't personally guarantee debts of the business
- Keep accurate financial and legal records
- Stay current with all licenses and permits

The checklist above may seem like overkill for a small business, but if your LLC should run into legal trouble, an attorney for the other party may look for any way that you pierced the corporate veil in order to bring your personal assets into play. You don't want to risk losing your home after someone slips on ice at your rental property simply because you regularly paid personal bills from your business checking account.

State LLC Created In
(Does not have to be your home state)

_____

LLC Creation Date

_____

Annual LLC Renewal Fee (if applicable)

_____

Due Date of Annual LLC Renewal

_____

▶ 4 Register Your Domain & Custom E-mail

If you plan to utilize a website for your business, now is a great time to register your domain and create a custom email address for your business. Use a site such as GoDaddy.com or Namecheap.com to register your domain. This typically takes less than 15 minutes and involves a small annual fee to secure the rights to the domain. If you found that you wanted to use a site such as "bestcompanyever.com", but that name has been taken, you could decide to purchase the name from the current owner (if that's an option), or choose another domain ending, such as ".net" or ".org".

Register your domain before choosing an email provider. Once you have ownership of your domain, you can create custom email addresses with your provider using your domain. This will look more professional to your future customers than using a generic Gmail address.

Using customized email addresses also helps with marketing. Customers will remember your business better when your business name is in everything they see regarding your products and contact information (website, email, social media handles, etc).

Domain Provider

_____

Registration Fee

_____

Registration Expiration Date

_____

Email Provider

_____

▶ 5 Get Your Employer Identification Number (EIN)

Registering for an Employer Identification Number (EIN) with the IRS is simple and FREE. Make sure that you do this directly via the IRS website. If you do a Google search, third-party sites often pop up that charge a fee for registering for this number. This is an unnecessary expense. The IRS website is user-friendly and it will provide you with your EIN immediately upon submission of the application. You can download a copy of the PDF letter to keep in your permanent files. *Don't lose this paper as you'll need it for opening bank accounts and for other legal purposes.*

- **Confirm you need an EIN** - Solo LLCs or sole proprietors without employees can use their Social Security Number (SSN) for taxes, but an EIN adds a professional layer. The EIN may be needed for banking purposes, hiring employees, or keeping personal and business assets separate.
- **Head to the IRS website** - Go to irs.gov and search "Apply for an EIN" or jump straight to irs.gov/businesses/small-businesses-self-employed/apply-for-an-employer-identification-number-ein-online
- **Pick your business type** - Choose sole proprietor if you chose not to create an LLC, or LLC if you have incorporated your business at the state level.
- **Fill in the details and answer a few questions**
- **Choose how to receive your EIN** - If you choose to receive it electronically, you'll receive it immediately and can download a PDF for your files. If you choose to receive it via USPS, it can take weeks for

- the IRS to send this (and you risk having it get lost in the mail).
- **Submit and save your number** - After submitting, you'll see a confirmation with your 9-digit EIN (e.g., 12-3456789). Print out a copy and place it in a safe place and save a copy of the PDF in a secure location.

Employer Identification Number (EIN)

---

6 ▶ Set Up Phone Number and/or PO Box

Every business needs a way for customers to get in touch with them, right? E-mail is great, but a phone and/or text number may also be necessary for your business.

These days it's relatively inexpensive and easy to get phone numbers and post office boxes online. This is a great way to separate yourself from the business outside of operating hours. You can create a business phone number that goes straight to your cell phone, but turn off the ringer on the weekends or while you're on vacation. In the same vein, it's a good idea to have mail going to a PO Box if you won't have a brick and mortar building where customers or clients visit.

Phone Number - Check out sites like Google Voice, Grasshopper, or TextNow for free or inexpensive phone numbers. Download an app to hook up to your new phone number and you're ready to contact your first customer. And don't forget to turn Do Not Disturb on during your out of office hours. Being available 24/7 is not sustainable and can give clients the impression that contacting you on the weekends or during dinner with your family is allowed. Create good habits for you and your clients early on.

PO Box - You can now register for a PO Box online as well. Simply go to usps.com, click "Quick Tools," then "Rent or Renew a PO Box," or jump straight to usps.com/pobox. Choose a location near you, a box size, and a rental term. Complete the remaining information, pay online and you're almost done! You just need to visit the post office within 30 days to show your ID and pick up your keys.

f you need additional services, such as mail forwarding, scanning, 24/7 delivery, or UPS package delivery, utilizing the services of The UPS Store might better fit your needs. Check with your local store to compare costs and services with your local post office.

Phone Number

_____

Provider

_____

Monthly/Annual Cost (& renewal date if applicable)

_____

PO Box Number

_____

Length of Contract & Cost

_____

7 ▶ Open Your Bank Account(s)

One of the most important tasks to complete for a new business is opening a business bank account. Start off simply with one checking account. You can always add others (such as a savings account, or a separate account for processing payroll) later. As mentioned earlier, separation of your business and personal assets is key in maintaining the legal liability protection with an LLC.

Running your income and expenses exclusively through your business bank account also creates a more stable financial position. It's easier to summarize your income and expenses for financial review and tax preparation if all activity within a bank account is strictly business related. If you (or your accountant) have to wonder whether an Amazon or Walmart receipt is for business purposes, you're risking the loss of valuable tax deductions.

You're also giving the IRS more leeway in reviewing all of your personal accounts if they see personal expenses being paid through your business account.

They'll roll up their sleeves to see if there are non-business expenses deducted on your tax return.

You can set up your bank account online in a matter of minutes now. If you don't feel the need for a local branch, you may have more options to choose from. Banks like Bluevine or Novo are new players that cater to online businesses. Or you could opt for a more traditional bank, if they offer the services you'll need.

- Choose a bank based on the services they offer and their fee structure
- Gather the documents & information you've created for your business thus far
  - business proof, such as LLC Articles of Organization, business license, or sole proprietor dba
  - employer identification number (EIN)
  - driver's license or passport
  - business address
- Complete the online application to open your account
- Fund your account

Bank Name

_____

Routing Number (9 Digit) & Account Number

_____

Monthly Fee

_____

Will you need to order paper checks?

_____

Apply for a business credit card now as well. You'll want to use a credit card for certain purchases (such as online subscriptions). This will allow you to keep all of your business transactions separate from your personal.

8 ▶ Register with Your Payment Provider(s)

If you will sell items online, or accept electronic payments from customers, you'll need to register for an online payment provider, in addition to creating your operating bank account.

Some of the most popular payment providers are:

- PayPal
- Stripe
- Square
- Venmo
- Shopify
- Apple Pay
- Google Pay
- Cash App

Perform a quick online search to compare the services and fees of each. Determine whether they work with your business bank. Some may work more seamlessly with certain banks than others. Credit card processing fees can add up, but they're now a cost of doing business and can keep account receivable to a minimum.

Registering for an online payment account is similar to setting up your online bank account. The difference comes at the end when you link your business account to the payment processor. The payment processor will ask for the same legal documents as your bank in order to verify the existence of your business and your personal identity. It will then connect with your bank so you can easily transfer your sales receipts from the payment processor to your business checking account.

Important Note - If you are using software such as QuickBooks or Wave to track your business finances, make sure any transfers between your payment processor and your checking account are recorded as "transfers" and not "deposits" as this could result in doubling-up the income on your financials and causing you to pay too much in tax at the end of the year.

Use the table below to research several payment providers and their fees. These fees can really add up as your sales grow, so it's important to budget these into your financial plans.

Processor	Monthly Fee	Processing Fee

Chosen Payment Provider

_____

Account Number

_____

9 ▶ Rent Business Space

If your business will require you to secure a brick and mortar space, you should now have all the legal and financial documents you need to secure a lease in the business name. Unless you have already had your eye on the perfect space, this is one task you may not be able to complete right away. But at least you know you have what you'll need when that space becomes available!

If your business will require you to secure a brick and mortar space, you should now have all the legal and financial documents you need to secure a lease in the business name. Unless you have already had your eye on the perfect space, this is one task you may not be able to complete right away. But at least you know you have what you'll need when that space becomes available!

Remember to put the lease in the business name if you decided to go the LLC route. And make all rent payments from your business bank account. If you have to pay a deposit on the space, transfer the cash from your personal account to your business bank account, and then pay the deposit from your business account. You won't pay tax on this deposit, but this transfer makes it easier for your accountant to track money you've contributed to the business. This could be very important come tax season.

Landlord Name & Address

_____

Lease Length & Monthly Rent

_____

Location Address

_____

Chapter Four

Choosing the Ideal Business Structure

You've been watching the marketing videos, creating your funnels, and designing your product. You're all set to sell your product and then the realities of setting up your business sets in. Should you be a sole proprietor, LLC, or partnership? And what is the magic behind an S-Corporation you keep hearing about?

There is no right answer for every situation, hence the different entity types available. Some entities allow more flexibility, while others focus on tax savings once the business has grown enough to have a tax problem at year-end. Some entrepreneurs have one business venture structured as an S-Corp and others structured as an LLC taxed as a partnership. There are pro's and con's to each, depending on the particular circumstances a business owner might be facing, so make this decision carefully with the assistance of both your attorney and your CPA.

There are a lot of advertisements claiming that you can save more in taxes by choosing one entity over another. Before you get caught up in the hype, keep in mind that tax savings should only be one piece of the puzzle in any decision-making conversations you have regarding your business over the years. I had a large client buy into the S-Corporation hype, despite my warnings that it wasn't the right decision for their partnership and pay structure. It saved taxes in the short-term, but they got a rude awakening when a shareholder left and took 33% of the business with them. The tax savings were nothing compared to the cash paid out when that individual left the organization and took advantage of the shares of stock they owned after just 3 years with the business.

Choose an entity structure that keeps your accounting and tax situation as simple and flexible as possible in the beginning, while also providing legal protection and tax savings opportunities. If you have the right conversations with qualified professionals up front, you can minimize your tax burden, but also plan appropriately for the future.

Business entity structures range from the simplest sole proprietorship to a corporation owned by stockholders. Review the basics of each type, as well as the pro's and con's. Use the included worksheets to note questions for your particular business and to have more meaningful discussions with your advisors in making a final decision that best suits your needs.

By the Numbers

According to the SBA a small business is defined as one having fewer than 500 employees. The vast majority of businesses with no employees are sole proprietorships, while just over half of those with employees are formed as S-corporations (source Statistics of US Businesses 2017, US Census Bureau). S-

Corporations are extremely popular, due to the potential for tax savings for the owners, but the Tax Cuts and Jobs Act of 2017 (TCJA) created some tax savings opportunities that have made the sole proprietorship or LLC's more advantageous in some instances, which allows solopreneurs to keep things simplified while also enjoying some tax benefits that weren't available before.

NON-EMPLOYER FIRMS

86.6% Sole Proprietorship

SMALL EMPLOYER FIRMS

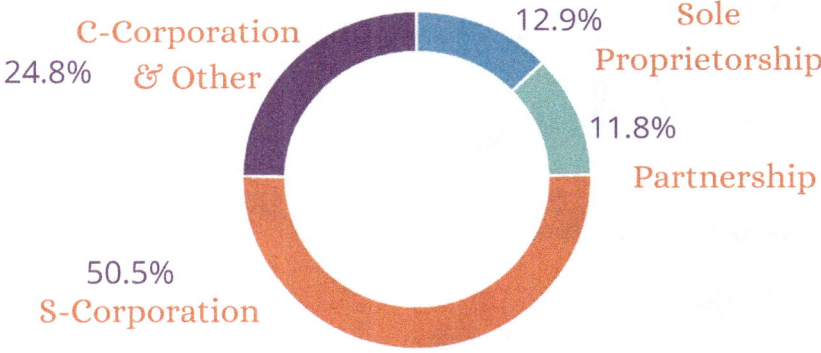

C-Corporation & Other 24.8%

12.9% Sole Proprietorship

11.8% Partnership

50.5% S-Corporation

Sole Proprietorship

A sole proprietorship is the simplest structure for a solopreneur to follow. Many individuals may already be operating one of these without knowing it due to the explosion of activity in the gig economy. You still need to pay tax on all of your earnings, and you need to acquire all of the necessary licenses required in your line of work, but you can also deduct business expenses related to this activity. This is far and away the entity used by most individuals working independently, with no employees.

- Easy and inexpensive to start up and operate
- No separate legal filings required to begin operations
- Owner has complete control over operations and all decision-making
- No separate corporate income tax return to file as all income and expenses are reported on the owner's Form 1040 via a Schedule C
- Owners can deduct all ordinary and necessary business expenses, as well as health insurance premiums and retirement contributions
- No payroll tax filings to complete as there are no employees and sole proprietors are not permitted to be on payroll without forming a separate legal entity

Con's

- Owners have unlimited legal liability from customers or other third parties
- Personal and business financing can be difficult to acquire as lenders see these as unstable sources of income
- Owners are responsible for making quarterly estimated tax payments on earnings or risk IRS penalties and interest, which can be a budgeting learning curve for many
- Sole proprietors tend to wear many hats due to lack of partners or employees to help manage the business and all of the decision-making

Partnership

A partnership is an entity comprised of two or more individuals agreeing to go into business with one another. Partnerships are required to be registered at the state level and a formal partnership agreement should be drafted with the assistance of an attorney to spell out how certain situations will be handled, such as admitting new partners, buying out retiring partners, splitting profits and losses and handling other legal matters that may arise during the course of running the business.

Pro's

- Partners aren't personally liable for business debts or liabilities as long as the partnership is formed as a Limited Partnership (LP), a Limited Liability Partnership (LLP), or a Limited Liability Corporation (LLC)
- Partners can bring different areas of expertise and varying skill sets to the table
- Partnerships allow for flexibility in admitting new partners as the need arises
- Profits, losses, and capital accounts can all be shared at varying percentages to allow for equitable financial arrangements, and these can be changed by the partners by simply amending the partnership agreement
- Capital contribution needs are shared by multiple individuals

- There are multiple individuals and personalities making business decisions, which makes communication, legal agreements and meshing of personalities very important
- Partners are not permitted to pay themselves payroll and are responsible for making quarterly estimated tax payments on earnings or risk IRS penalties and interest
- Profits are shared by all partners, which may be a change for someone used to keeping all the profits for themselves
- Additional tax forms must be filed to report the partnership earnings and each individual partner's share of profits, losses, and capital

S-Corporation

An S-corporation is not a specific legal entity choice, but rather a tax election notifying the IRS that the LLC or partnership is requesting to be taxed under what can be more favorable S-corporation tax rules. An S-Corporation shareholder can be a passive owner, or wear the hat of both an employee and and investor if they also work in the business. If this is the case, the shareholder will receive both a W-2 for wages earned while working in the business and a Schedule K-1 showing their share of profits or losses generated by the business for the year.

- S-corporations provide protection from business liabilities and debts for shareholders
- Shareholders own stock in the business and can be passive investors or employees of the corporation
- Unlike partnerships, shareholders actively working in the business can receive wages
- There may be opportunities for more pension and profit sharing options, depending on pension and tax laws
- Earnings over and above reasonable compensation for shareholders are not subject to FICA tax as they are considered investment earnings

Con's

- Shareholders working within the business must take reasonable wages, so a solopreneur with no other employees is tasked with the burden and cost of running payroll for themselves and filing quarterly and annual payroll tax forms
- Limited to one class of stock, which may limit opportunities for enticing outside investors
- Number of shareholders is limited to 100
- Shareholder distributions and earnings must be allocated based on ownership percentage, thus removing the flexibility enjoyed with partnerships
- Losses can only be taken to the extent of shareholder basis
- Additional tax forms must be filed to report the corporate earnings & each individual shareholder's earnings/losses on a K-1

C-Corporation

A corporation is unique from the other entities discussed as it is a separate taxpaying entity and responsible for paying its own taxes on all earnings not distributed by year-end. Individuals can still work within the organization and own stock, but there are no K-1s issues. Employees receive W-2s for all wage earnings. If dividends are declared and paid by the board of directors, earnings on that income is paid by the individual stockholders.

Pro's

- Protection from business liabilities and debts for shareholders
- Can have an unlimited number of shareholders
- Can provide multiple classes of stock to entice investors
- Able to go public in order to raise capital needed for growth
- Easier to secure financing as capital needs arise
- Dividends and capital gains realized on the sale of appreciated stock currently enjoy more favorable tax rates than some other forms of income
- More opportunities may be available for profit sharing options for profitable businesses
- Lower corporate tax rate as the TCJA lowered the corporate tax rate to 21% for earnings left in the corporation

- Corporations pay taxations on profits not paid out as wages at the end of the year, which can lead to double-taxation
- Corporations require a separate tax return, and can be more costly and complex to set-up and administer
- Stockholder meetings must be held at least annually and minutes must be kept on file to adhere to state and federal regulations

Limited Liability Corporation (LLC)

An LLC is an extremely popular legal entity choice for many solopreneurs and partnerships as it can add an additional layer of legal protection not offered by sole proprietorships and general partnerships.

Deciding to be an LLC is more of a legal decision than a tax decision. The IRS taxes an LLC based on the underlying structure of the entity without the LLC filing. An LLC is organized at the state level and may be required to pay an annual filing fee to the state. Owners in an LLC are referred to as "members" and earnings flow through to their personal tax return, the same as it would in a sole proprietorship, partnership or S-corporation.

Single Member LLCs (SMLLC)

- A sole proprietorship can register with the state to be recognized as an LLC for legal liability protection purposes
- This is a popular decision for rental property owners or individuals concerned with the possibility of being sued in their line of business
- The IRS disregards an LLC with only one owner and all tax filings are the same as with a sole proprietorship
- Wages are still disallowed for a SMLLC
- A single-member LLC can elect to be taxed as an S-Corporation if earnings and other factors indicate that this would be a wise financial and tax savings decision

Multi-Member LLC (Partnership)

- An LLC with multiple members is taxed as a partnership by the IRS
- An LLC taxed as a partnership can elect to be taxed as an S-corporation to take advantage of those tax laws and possible tax savings, if tax planning indicates that the costs outweigh the additional costs and filing burdens

Choosing An Entity

As you make an entity choice decision, spend some time answering the questions below. They can provide insight for you and your professional team so you come to the most appropriate choice for your business needs.

Will you be operating independently (as a sole proprietor) or will there be partners involved?

_____

_____

_____

_____

_____

Do you need the added layer of liability protection of an LLC based on your business activities?

_____

_____

_____

_____

_____

Do you anticipate hiring employees immediately, or in the near future?

_____

_____

_____

_____

Do you handle your finances in a way that you feel you will pay estimated taxes regularly and timely?

_____

_____

_____

_____

_____

If there will be partners involved, have you discussed how you will allocate profits and losses?

_____

_____

_____

_____

_____

If there are partners involved, is flexibility in determining allocations of profit & losses required?

_____

_____

_____

_____

_____

Will receiving W-2 income assist in requesting lending?

_____

_____

_____

_____

_____

Do you anticipate that your earnings will be such that an S-Corporation makes sense for tax savings after taking a reasonable salary?

_____

_____

_____

_____

_____

If you were hired to perform your duties for another corporation, what would you consider reasonable compensation for your role?

_____

_____

_____

_____

_____

Chapter Five

All About LLCs

Limited Liability Companies (LLCs) are governed by the laws of the state in which they are created. Just as each state has its own laws regarding employment practices, speed limits, and rental properties, there are also individual state regulations and guidelines for creating and operating an LLC.

Before you make a decision regarding whether or not an LLC is the right legal decision for your business, do yourself a favor and forget every Instagram or TikTok video you've ever seen telling you that creating an LLC will save you taxes. An LLC is a LEGAL protection tool and does not play a role in which expenses you can and cannot deduct. You can deduct the same exact expenses as a sole proprietor that you can deduct if your business is set up as an LLC.

The IRS treats LLCs as "disregarded entities". Simply put, the IRS ignores your legal status with your state for tax reporting purposes. Sole proprietors, single-member LLCs, and multi-member LLCs (partnerships) are all able to deduct reasonable and ordinary business expenses on their tax returns. *(More on the definitions of ordinary and necessary expenses in another chapter.)*

You should always consult with an attorney in creating an LLC. They can best advise you on creating articles of incorporation and other documents that will protect your business and personal assets should a business-related lawsuit arise. It would be an unfortunate situation if an attorney easily poked holes in your legal protection because you didn't have proper documents filed or didn't act like a separate entity, allowing the courts to find you personally liable.

An attorney is especially helpful when starting a business with a partner. In addition to the basic set-up documentation, they can guide you through the tough conversations surrounding ownership percentages, partner roles, and how to handle the exit of a partner due to life changes, disagreements, or death.

Partnerships start out on a positive note, or they wouldn't start at all. The individuals are excited to bring a product to market or start their own service business. However, There can be unrealistic expectations by one or more parties that don't come to light until the dust has settled and the day-to-day work begins. A good partnership agreement can help iron out wrinkles before they become deal-breakers. Having a solid document to refer to can take the emotion out of these conversations so you can still enjoy Thanksgiving dinners as family members or weekend fishing trips as friends without allowing the business to ruin close relationships.

Reasons for Creating an LLC

As I mentioned above, you do not need to create an LLC in order to deduct legitimate business expenses. However, an LLC can provide peace of mind and structure for your business. It is often well worth an upfront investment to protect your assets in the long run. Below are some of the most common reasons that small business owners have when deciding to protect their assets behind the shield of an LLC:

✓ Protection from personal liability when signing contracts

✓ Formalizing roles and determining ownership percentages with multiple owners

✓ Protection from illegal or harmful acts performed by employees

✓ Establishing credibility with third parties

✓ Applying for loans or look for outside investors

✓ Protection of intellectual property

Additional Tasks Associated with an LLC

When you create an LLC, it's a good idea to think of it as a separate living, breathing entity. Congratulations! You're now the proud new owner of something that will bring joy, tears, sleepless nights, and probably some debt along the way. But hopefully the success you find outweighs all of the angst and overwhelm that you will feel in the beginning.

Any new parents (of either a human or fur baby) will tell you it's impossible to foresee the obstacles you'll face or decisions you'll find yourself making on a daily basis. The responsibilities can feel overwhelming, but there are some basics you can take note of so you feel more confident in keeping the business healthy and growing:

✓ File annual reports with your state (fees and filing requirements vary by state

✓ Contracts, rental, and loan agreements should be created in the LLC name

✓ All assets (including cash and bank accounts) should be separated from the personal assets of the owner(s)

It is imperative to keep all cash and other assets separate between business & personal activity. Otherwise, you risk piercing the corporate veil & losing legal protections.

Taxation of LLCs

Although the IRS treats LLCs as disregarded entities for tax purposes, there are different forms that need to be filed, based on whether there is one owner, multiple owners, or the LLC has elected to be taxed as an S-Corporation:

Single-Member LLC

- The LLC is a disregarded entity for IRS purposes
- Business income and expenses are reported on Schedule C of the member's Form 1040
- The owner is self-employed for tax purposes
- The owner must make estimated tax payments to cover tax on the income earned during the year

Multi-Member LLC

- The LLC is a disregarded entity for IRS purposes
- Business income and expenses are reported on Form 1065 (partnership tax return)
- Ordinary business income to partners is generally considered self-employed income for tax purposes
- Each partner is taxed on their share of income based on the partnership agreement (partners will receive a form K-1 from the partnership allocating their share of income or loss)
- Net income (or loss) flows through the partnership to the members' Forms 1040 via K-1s on the Form 1065
- The partners must make estimated tax payments to cover tax on their share of the income earned during the year
- A partnership can inadvertently be formed if spouses create a business in a non-community property state and don't file a qualified joint venture election with the IRS

S-Corporation Election

- An S-corporation is formed when an LLC files an election with the IRS to take advantage of S-corporation tax laws
- Business income and expenses are reported on Form 1120-S (S-corporation tax return)
- Shareholders are treated as employees **and** shareholders for tax purposes (they will receive a W-2 and a K-1 from the business to properly allocate earnings)
- Taxes on earnings are paid in via quarterly estimated tax payments and/or W-2 withholdings

Partnerships have much more flexibility in allocating business income and loss than an S-corporation and partnership agreements can be changed as needed to meet the changing roles and contributions of partners. S-corporations have much more rigid taxation and allocation rules to follow. All distributions and earnings must be allocated based on the individual's ownership percentage of shares in the business. Despite tax-savings opportunities available, an S-corporation isn't the right decision for all businesses. Slow-walk your election decision and review tax-planning with your CPA carefully before making a final decision.

Simply purchasing an asset in the LLC name won't automatically make it 100% deductible for the business. The IRS will review how it is used and will prorate business deductions vs personal-use accordingly.

Chapter Six

Create Simple Financials that Drive Your Profits

One of the biggest stressors new small business owners face is handling their finances. You're not a CPA. How can anyone (especially the IRS) expect you to get all of this right and figure out taxes at the end of the year?!

Don't let the overwhelm of bookkeeping hold you back from reaching your goals. As scary as numbers can be, they are imperative in understanding what is working and what isn't. And they'll help bankers decide whether or not to lend you money for new projects or growth opportunities.

Your numbers are important in determining how much you'll owe on your tax return. But that should be the end of your financial review process, not the beginning.

Your financial statements (even basic ones) can let you know if you can afford to hire an employee, if you are losing money on a particular product, or if certain expenses are creeping up each year and need to be reviewed.

Balance Sheet

This report is called a balance sheet because everything in accounting is a two step process. Money that makes your bank balance go down makes your expense account go up. This system was widely used by the Medici Bank as far back as the 1300s. It was so successful it became widely adopted by other businesses and banks and is still the way we handle business finances today.

A balance sheet is simply a photo taken of your business in one moment of time that shows how healthy it is financially. Put quite simply, it tells the reader (typically your lender or other investor) whether your business owns more than it owes.

That can change daily, which is why it is a snapshot of your business. If you have a large credit card bill due on Monday, the business may not look very healthy. But then you make a large sale on Wednesday and pay that credit card in full. Your balance sheet would tell a different story about your business on Wednesday than it did on Monday.

Also, you could have a large bill due to a vendor, but you also have a large amount of inventory on hand. One is something your business owns (inventory), the other is something your business owes (vendor bill), but they zero each other out on the balance sheet, so things are currently staying positively balanced.

Assets

Assets are what your business owns. Assets typically consist of:

- Cash in Banks
- Accounts Receivable (what customers owe you)
- Inventory (products on hand to sell)
- Buildings
- Equipment
- Vehicles

EXAMPLE

Alex is setting up her beachside stand to sell her jewelry. Everything she brings with her would be an asset. She has the following:

Cash in her bank account $5,000

Tiki Hut $1,500 (cost to build)

Equipment $1,000 cell phone
$850 laptop

Vehicle $3,500 golf cart

Inventory $3,000 (cost to purchase/create)

Accounts Receivable $800 (payments due from sales she made the week before)

Alex's total assets on the day she opens her business are $15,650.

Track Your Assets

Now let's list the assets you have in your business:

Cash in Checking Account _____

Cash in Savings Account _____

Cash on Hand _____

**Building (if owned
by business)** _____

Equipment _____ _____

_____ _____

_____ _____

_____ _____

Vehicle (if owned by business) _____

Inventory _____

Accounts Receivable _____

TOTAL OF YOUR ASSETS: _____

Note on Inventory:
Value this at your cost,
not what you will sell it
for. If Alex purchased 3
bracelets @ $15 each to
resell later, her bracelet
inventory would be $45.

Liabilities (Debts)

Liabilities are what your business owes to others.

Liabilities typically consist of:

- Accounts Payable (invoices due to vendors)
- Credit Cards
- Bank Loans
- Family/Friend Loans

EXAMPLE

Alex didn't have cash immediately available to start her business, so she has some liabilities she will need to pay down as her sales improve:

Accounts Payable $1,200 (for inventory)

Credit Card $300 (due on her Chase card)

Bank Loan $2,850 (for golf cart)

Family/Friend Loan $2,500 (loan from mom)

Alex's total liabilities on the day she opens her business are $6,850.

Track Your Liabilities

Now let's list the liabilities you have in your business:

Accounts Payable

_____   _____
_____   _____
_____   _____
_____   _____

Credit Card(s)

_____   _____
_____   _____

Bank Loan(s)

_____   _____
_____   _____

Family/Friend Loan   _____

TOTAL OF YOUR LIABILITIES: _____

Note on Loans:
List these at the balance shown on your statement (what it would take to pay them off today).

Owner's Equity

If you sold the business and paid off all the debts, this is what you could take home.

Assets (+) less Liabilities (-) = Owner's Equity

As your assets increase, so does the value of your business (equity).

As your liabilities increase, the value of your business decreases because you'll have to use assets later to pay off vendors or lenders.

Assets - Liabilities = Owner's Equity

Alex has $8,800 in owner's equity in her business. If she closed her bank accounts, sold her assets, and collected her accounts receivable, she'd have $8,800 left to take home after she paid off her loans, vendors, and credit cards.

Assets - $15,650 - Liabilities $6,850 = $8,800 Owner's Equity

Calculate Your Owner's Equity

What is your business worth to you today?

(A) Take the total of your assets from your asset worksheet.

(B) Subtract the total of your debts from your liability worksheet.

(C) This is what you would likely walk away with if you sold your business today and decided to focus on another venture.

Assets - _____ (A)
Liabilities _____ (B) = _____ (C) Owner's Equity

Note on Equity:
You could have negative equity in your business if your liabilities are more than your assets. You may risk having to put in personal funds to cover business debts.

Income Statement

The income statement is what most small business owners focus on. This is a summary of all the money your business has made (sales) and all the money the business has spent (expenses).

In a healthy business, your sales will outweigh your expenses so you can earn a paycheck and pay yourself at the end of the day.

Don't fall into the trap of trying to spend every dollar you earn so you won't owe taxes at the end of the year. Sure, you could give Amazon all of your hard-earned money and short-change the IRS. But you're also short-changing yourself and your family at the same time. Did you really start this business to become an unpaid laborer?

Taxes are unfortunately a fact of life. Do your best to minimize them, but focus on maximizing your income and becoming financially free before worrying about the IRS. Many a business owner has closed their doors because they let the fear of the IRS cause them to make poor spending decisions. Running a successful business is hard enough. Don't become a failed business statistic because the IRS boogey man kept you awake at night.

Income (Sales)

If you are a small business, track your income and sales on the cash basis. Simply put, this means money into the bank account less money out of the bank account equals your net income.

Your sales would include both cash sales and electronic sales that may go through PayPal, Stripe, Square, etc. Those deposits may take a day or two to hit your bank account, but include those as sales on your tax return and income statement. The delay isn't truly an accounts receivable situation. It's just a timing lag in transferring from one bank account to another.

EXAMPLE

Alex made both cash sales and electronic sales in her first week in business at her new beach location. She should look at both her cash receipts and her online payment accounts to verify her total sales.

Cash Sales $275

Electronic Sales $1,125 (gross before
                                  deduction of Square
                                  processing fees)

Alex's total sales for the week are $1,400.

Record sales at your **GROSS** figure before any deductions for fees. Record your fees separately.

Cost of Sales

If you are selling a product, your cost of sales is the direct cost of the product you are selling. If you are selling jewelry, as Alex is, this would include the cost of materials for any you created, the cost of any manufactured jewelry you purchased to resell, and any shipping costs you incurred when ordering the product.

Only record the cost of your sales as you sell an item. Place your item into your inventory figure on your balance sheet when you purchase it and then move it to your cost of sales on your income statement when you sell it.

The importance of inventory - It can be tempting to deduct your inventory as you purchase it so you show a bigger loss on your income statement and owe less tax at the end of the year. But what goes around comes around. You may have a big loss the first year because you have minimal sales and lots of inventory purchases. But next year when you sell that inventory you'll have to pay tax on that income anyway. You've already deducted the cost of the jewelry you sold, so your loss is overstated in year 1 and your income is overstated in year 2.

Tracking inventory and deducting it when the item is actually sold evens out your tax burden, and shows a more accurate picture of how much money you're making in your business.

Alex is starting out simply by having one bracelet to sell in various colors. Each bracelet costs her the same, so her inventory is simple. She is selling the bracelets for $50 each.

Beginning Inventory	$3,000 (200 bracelets @ $15)
Sales	$1,400 (28 bracelets @50)
Cost of Sales	**$420 (28 bracelets @ $15)**
Ending Inventory	$2,580 (172 bracelets @ $15)

So far, Alex's income statement is very simple. She has her total sales less the cost of those bracelets she has sold. This is referred to as your **gross profit.**

Cash Sales	$275
Electronic Sales	$1,125
Total Sales	**$1,400**
Less: Cost of Sales	($420)
Gross Profit	**$980**

Operating Expenses

Like all businesses, Alex also has operating costs to cover. Operating expenses are those that a business has regardless of the products or services sold. They are the expenses you incur to run your business and keep the doors open.

Advertising	$40
Credit Card Fees (2.5% of sales)	$28
Internet	$15
Office Supplies	$45
Rent *(her space on the beach)*	$75

Total Operating Expenses   **$203**

Alex's Net Income Statement

Cash Sales	$275
Electronic Sales	$1,125
Total Sales	**$1,400**
Less: Cost of Sales	($420)
Gross Profit	**$980**
Operating Expenses	
Advertising	$40
Credit Card Fees (2.5% of sales)	$28
Internet	$15
Office Supplies	$45
Rent (her space on the beach)	$75
Total Operating Expenses	**($203)**
Net Income	**$777**

If you are using a product such as QuickBooks or Wave, they will automatically format your income and expenses for you as you input your bank and credit card transactions. If you record your transactions accurately, they will show you both your balance sheet and your income statement so you can track the health of your business and your net income on a daily/weekly/monthly basis.

Setting Up Bookkeeping Systems

When you first start out, keep things simple. You'll thank yourself in the long run. It can be tempting to set up QuickBooks, but if you don't need payroll or invoicing, and you're simply tracking income and expenses, it may be overwhelming. The more overwhelming your bookkeeping becomes, the less likely you are to stay on top of it.

That frustration can cost you money in the long run. You'll miss out on tax deductions if your expenses aren't tracked accurately and you may not pivot as quickly as you should if a particular product or service is costing you money, rather than making you money.

Keeping It Simple

If you want to keep it simple (and less expensive) a good spreadsheet can do the trick. If you use a spreadsheet, track your income and expenses by month and leave a column to indicate the type of income or expense. This will allow you to add up all the common expenses (such as office supplies or subscriptions) for a month or year.

If you just have a running check register, you'll see your bank balance, but you won't see a quick summary of where the money went. How much did you spend on office supplies? Are your online subscriptions getting out hand? Make sure your system is giving you detailed information at a glance so you can make informed decisions. Your financials should be one of the first tools you review to see if you're on track to be profitable and sustainable.

Below is are snapshots of a Google Sheet that I use with clients that takes very basic data entry from a monthly tab and summarizes it into a profit and loss. The monthly tabsallow for basic entry of date, payee, amount, and type of expense. The figures then flow to to a summary page that shows totals for each month and year-to-date. This is proof that you can create simple, yet powerful, tools with inexpensive software.

Home Base — PROFIT AND LOSS REPORT
For the Year Ended December 31, 2025

	Year-To-Date	January	February	March	April	May	June	July	August	September	October	November	December
Income													
Sales	0.00	0.00	0.00	0.00	0.00	0.00	0.00	0.00	0.00	0.00	0.00	0.00	0.00
Other Income	0.00	0.00	0.00	0.00	0.00	0.00	0.00	0.00	0.00	0.00	0.00	0.00	0.00
Interest Income	0.00	0.00	0.00	0.00	0.00	0.00	0.00	0.00	0.00	0.00	0.00	0.00	0.00
Customer Refunds	0.00	0.00	0.00	0.00	0.00	0.00	0.00	0.00	0.00	0.00	0.00	0.00	0.00
TOTAL INCOME	0.00	0.00	0.00	0.00	0.00	0.00	0.00	0.00	0.00	0.00	0.00	0.00	0.00
Cost of Sales													
Commissions	0.00	0.00	0.00	0.00	0.00	0.00	0.00	0.00	0.00	0.00	0.00	0.00	0.00
Inventory/Materials	0.00	0.00	0.00	0.00	0.00	0.00	0.00	0.00	0.00	0.00	0.00	0.00	0.00
Payment Processor Fees	0.00	0.00	0.00	0.00	0.00	0.00	0.00	0.00	0.00	0.00	0.00	0.00	0.00
Permits	0.00	0.00	0.00	0.00	0.00	0.00	0.00	0.00	0.00	0.00	0.00	0.00	0.00
Shipping	0.00	0.00	0.00	0.00	0.00	0.00	0.00	0.00	0.00	0.00	0.00	0.00	0.00
Shipping Supplies	0.00	0.00	0.00	0.00	0.00	0.00	0.00	0.00	0.00	0.00	0.00	0.00	0.00
TOTAL COST OF SALES	0.00	0.00	0.00	0.00	0.00	0.00	0.00	0.00	0.00	0.00	0.00	0.00	0.00
General Expenses													
Advertising	0.00	0.00	0.00	0.00	0.00	0.00	0.00	0.00	0.00	0.00	0.00	0.00	0.00
Bank Fees	0.00	0.00	0.00	0.00	0.00	0.00	0.00	0.00	0.00	0.00	0.00	0.00	0.00
Charitable Contributions	0.00	0.00	0.00	0.00	0.00	0.00	0.00	0.00	0.00	0.00	0.00	0.00	0.00
Dues	0.00	0.00	0.00	0.00	0.00	0.00	0.00	0.00	0.00	0.00	0.00	0.00	0.00
Education & Training	0.00	0.00	0.00	0.00	0.00	0.00	0.00	0.00	0.00	0.00	0.00	0.00	0.00
Equipment Lease/Rentals	0.00	0.00	0.00	0.00	0.00	0.00	0.00	0.00	0.00	0.00	0.00	0.00	0.00
Gifts (Customers/Employees)	0.00	0.00	0.00	0.00	0.00	0.00	0.00	0.00	0.00	0.00	0.00	0.00	0.00
Insurance - General	0.00	0.00	0.00	0.00	0.00	0.00	0.00	0.00	0.00	0.00	0.00	0.00	0.00
Insurance - Health	0.00	0.00	0.00	0.00	0.00	0.00	0.00	0.00	0.00	0.00	0.00	0.00	0.00
Interest	0.00	0.00	0.00	0.00	0.00	0.00	0.00	0.00	0.00	0.00	0.00	0.00	0.00
Internet	0.00	0.00	0.00	0.00	0.00	0.00	0.00	0.00	0.00	0.00	0.00	0.00	0.00
Laundry & Cleaning	0.00	0.00	0.00	0.00	0.00	0.00	0.00	0.00	0.00	0.00	0.00	0.00	0.00
Legal & Professional	0.00	0.00	0.00	0.00	0.00	0.00	0.00	0.00	0.00	0.00	0.00	0.00	0.00
Licenses	0.00	0.00	0.00	0.00	0.00	0.00	0.00	0.00	0.00	0.00	0.00	0.00	0.00
Meals	0.00	0.00	0.00	0.00	0.00	0.00	0.00	0.00	0.00	0.00	0.00	0.00	0.00
Miscellaneous	0.00	0.00	0.00	0.00	0.00	0.00	0.00	0.00	0.00	0.00	0.00	0.00	0.00
Office Supplies	0.00	0.00	0.00	0.00	0.00	0.00	0.00	0.00	0.00	0.00	0.00	0.00	0.00
Parking	0.00	0.00	0.00	0.00	0.00	0.00	0.00	0.00	0.00	0.00	0.00	0.00	0.00
Payroll Processing Fees	0.00	0.00	0.00	0.00	0.00	0.00	0.00	0.00	0.00	0.00	0.00	0.00	0.00
Payroll Taxes	0.00	0.00	0.00	0.00	0.00	0.00	0.00	0.00	0.00	0.00	0.00	0.00	0.00
Pension	0.00	0.00	0.00	0.00	0.00	0.00	0.00	0.00	0.00	0.00	0.00	0.00	0.00
Postage	0.00	0.00	0.00	0.00	0.00	0.00	0.00	0.00	0.00	0.00	0.00	0.00	0.00
Rent - Building	0.00	0.00	0.00	0.00	0.00	0.00	0.00	0.00	0.00	0.00	0.00	0.00	0.00
Repairs & Maintenance	0.00	0.00	0.00	0.00	0.00	0.00	0.00	0.00	0.00	0.00	0.00	0.00	0.00
Salaries & Wages	0.00	0.00	0.00	0.00	0.00	0.00	0.00	0.00	0.00	0.00	0.00	0.00	0.00
Small Tools & Equipment	0.00	0.00	0.00	0.00	0.00	0.00	0.00	0.00	0.00	0.00	0.00	0.00	0.00
Software Subscriptions	0.00	0.00	0.00	0.00	0.00	0.00	0.00	0.00	0.00	0.00	0.00	0.00	0.00
Supplies	0.00	0.00	0.00	0.00	0.00	0.00	0.00	0.00	0.00	0.00	0.00	0.00	0.00
Taxes	0.00	0.00	0.00	0.00	0.00	0.00	0.00	0.00	0.00	0.00	0.00	0.00	0.00
Telephone	0.00	0.00	0.00	0.00	0.00	0.00	0.00	0.00	0.00	0.00	0.00	0.00	0.00
Tolls	0.00	0.00	0.00	0.00	0.00	0.00	0.00	0.00	0.00	0.00	0.00	0.00	0.00
Trash Removal	0.00	0.00	0.00	0.00	0.00	0.00	0.00	0.00	0.00	0.00	0.00	0.00	0.00
Travel	0.00	0.00	0.00	0.00	0.00	0.00	0.00	0.00	0.00	0.00	0.00	0.00	0.00
Uniforms	0.00	0.00	0.00	0.00	0.00	0.00	0.00	0.00	0.00	0.00	0.00	0.00	0.00
Utilities	0.00	0.00	0.00	0.00	0.00	0.00	0.00	0.00	0.00	0.00	0.00	0.00	0.00
TOTAL GENERAL EXPENSES	0.00	0.00	0.00	0.00	0.00	0.00	0.00	0.00	0.00	0.00	0.00	0.00	0.00
NET INCOME(LOSS)	0.00	0.00	0.00	0.00	0.00	0.00	0.00	0.00	0.00	0.00	0.00	0.00	0.00
Home Office	0.00	0.00	0.00	0.00	0.00	0.00	0.00	0.00	0.00	0.00	0.00	0.00	0.00
Cell Phone (Business Use)	0.00	0.00	0.00	0.00	0.00	0.00	0.00	0.00	0.00	0.00	0.00	0.00	0.00
Home Internet (Business Use)	0.00	0.00	0.00	0.00	0.00	0.00	0.00	0.00	0.00	0.00	0.00	0.00	0.00
Mileage (Business Mileage)	0.00	0.00	0.00	0.00	0.00	0.00	0.00	0.00	0.00	0.00	0.00	0.00	0.00
Interest - Credit Card	0.00	0.00	0.00	0.00	0.00	0.00	0.00	0.00	0.00	0.00	0.00	0.00	0.00
Interest - Business Loan(s)	0.00	0.00	0.00	0.00	0.00	0.00	0.00	0.00	0.00	0.00	0.00	0.00	0.00
Charitable Contributions	0.00	0.00	0.00	0.00	0.00	0.00	0.00	0.00	0.00	0.00	0.00	0.00	0.00
50% Business Meals	0.00	0.00	0.00	0.00	0.00	0.00	0.00	0.00	0.00	0.00	0.00	0.00	0.00
TAXABLE BUSINESS INCOME	0.00	0.00	0.00	0.00	0.00	0.00	0.00	0.00	0.00	0.00	0.00	0.00	0.00

Need a simple, but powerful Google Sheet? You can grab this sheet at:

Going All In

If you prefer more automation, or will need more bells and whistles to run your business (such as invoicing or payroll), consider a tool such as QuickBooks Online. When deciding on this option, do yourself (and your CPA) a huge favor. Ask for help in getting it up and running. It will be an initial investment, but it's always cheaper to allow someone to set things up correctly than to have them fix things later. I can't tell you the number of times I've offered to set up QBO, only to have clients assure me that they'll figure it out. Nine times out of ten, they're waving the white flag after realizing there's more to it than they anticipated.

Here are some tips on utilizing QuickBooks Online efficiently and keeping it from becoming a nightmare that you're hiring someone to clean up later.

1. Only utilize the modules you need (don't worry about accounts receivable if you aren't invoicing customers through the system)
2. Use the modules you set up correctly (if you do use invoices, make sure you post deposits to the invoice or you'll have a messy "undeposited funds" situation to clean up)
3. Use a very basic chart of accounts. Only set up accounts that you need in your business. Don't be afraid to delete included accounts if they don't pertain to your business. Simple is always better.
4. Utilize bank feeds to automate data entry.
5. Reconcile your bank and credit card account(s) every month. This will ensure that the data in QuickBooks is accurate. AI does make mistakes!

Below is a basic chart of accounts that you can use when setting up QuickBooks (or any other accounting system). Intuit includes a pre-set chart of accounts that is often overkill for small businesses. I recommend deleting any you don't need to keep things simple and streamlined.

BASIC CHART OF ACCOUNTS

BALANCE SHEET	PROFIT & LOSS

Assets (What the business owns)

Bank
  Checking
  Savings
Other Current Assets
  Investments
Fixed Assets
  Building
  Equipment
  Vehicles
  Accumulated Depreciation

Income

Regular Income
  Service Revenue
  Sale of Product
Other Income
  Interest
  Dividends
  Gain or Loss on Sale of Assets

Liabilities (What the business owes)

Current Liabilities
  Credit Cards Payable
  Line of Credit Payable
  Payroll Taxes Payable
  Sales Tax Payable
Long-Term Liabilities
  Note Payable (make separate acct
    for each loan)

Cost of Sales

  Freight & Delivery
  Materials
  Salaries & Wages (related to sales)
  Supplies
  Subcontractors

Member's Equity

Single Member LLC
  Member's Contributions* (Money In)
  Member's Draw* (Money Out)
  Member's Capital
Multi-Member LLC (Partnership)
  Partner 1 Contributions
  Partner 2 Contributions
  Partner 1 Draws
  Partner 2 Draws
  Partner 1 Capital
  Partner 2 Capital

Expenses

  Advertising
  Auto (Actual or Mileage)
  Commissions
  Depreciation
  Dues & Subscriptions
  Insurance
  Interest
  Legal & Professional Fees
  Meals
  Office Supplies
  Rent (Building or Equipment)
  Repairs & Maintenance
  Taxes**
  Travel
  Utilities
  Wages**

Member Contributions - Cash the owner contributes to the business, or where to record expenses pd from the owner's personal bank account

Member Draws - Cash taken out of the business by the owner, including pmts of quarterly estimated taxes

**Quarterly estimates & member draws are not recorded as payroll or deducted on the profit & loss

Your Chart of Accounts

Using the chart of accounts on the previous page as a guide, create an initial chart of accounts for your business. Keep it simple and only include things specifically related to your business. Don't include personal credit cards or bank accounts and don't overly complicate your expense accounts. Anything you purchase from Staples can go into "office supplies", for example.

Account Name	*Account Type*

Accounting Checklist

Keeping on top of your bookkeeping is the easiest way to save taxes and your insanity. Input your income and expenses on a weekly basis and reconcile your bank account on a monthly basis. You may find that your accountant changes the account that items are posted to, but at least you'll have the data they need to review your income and expenses and guide you on tax savings and business growth opportunities.

- Input income and expense activity (weekly)
- Ensure all income and expenses are coded to the correct accounts (weekly)
- Reconcile bank and credit card accounts (monthly)
- Review income and expenses for areas of concern or celebration (monthly)
- Pay federal and state estimated taxes (quarterly)
- Meet with your accountant to review books and do tax planning (semi-annually)

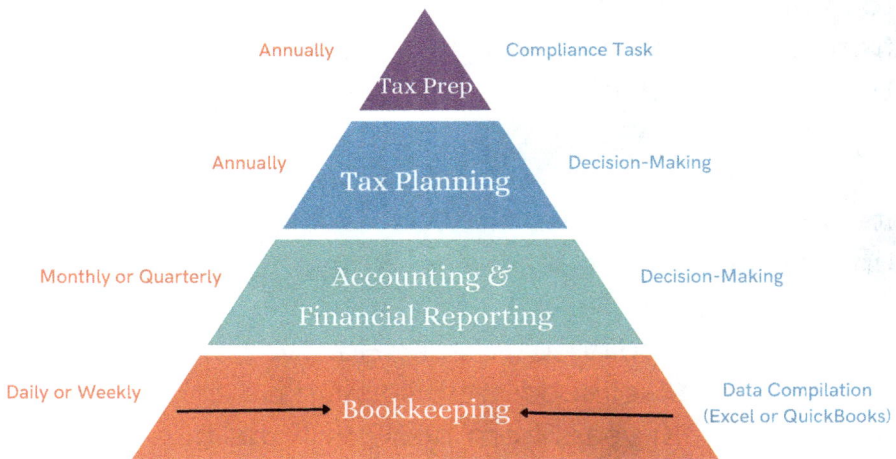

Annually — Tax Prep — Compliance Task

Annually — Tax Planning — Decision-Making

Monthly or Quarterly — Accounting & Financial Reporting — Decision-Making

Daily or Weekly — Bookkeeping — Data Compilation (Excel or QuickBooks)

Chapter Seven

Simplifying the Lending Process

As a small business owner, you may find that securing loans can be overwhelming, frustrating, and sometimes nearly impossible if you want reasonable interest rates and loan terms. Fair or not, banks are hesitant to lend to self-employed individuals. Income stemming from a W2 job is looked upon as more reliable and stable, whereas income from a business owned by one individual is considered high risk.

As an entrepreneur who has already invested countless dollars, sleepless nights, and days away from your family, the lending process can feel like adding insult to injury. You know how much harder it is to walk away from clients and a dream you've poured so much into, but from a bank's perspective it's all about the numbers.

It does make sense if you put yourself in the underwriter's shoes. If a friend or neighbor came to you for a loan, you'd probably have a list of questions. What is the money being used for? How will you repay it? What is the likelihood that you'll have the funds to repay it 5 or 10 years from now? Will the business still be around in several years to ensure the loan is repaid?

These are the same questions an underwriter will ask about you and your current financial situation.

Approval or Denial is Hidden in Your Numbers

It can be very hard to keep emotions out of the lending process, especially if the answer will determine a new product launch happening, or moving to a new location. An unknown third party holds your future in their hands and a loan denial can be crushing, at least in the short-term.

It can help to remember that your answer lies in your numbers. The stronger they are, the easier it is for an underwriter to approve your loan and have the funds waiting for you within a couple of days. Even if you use a friendly local bank, there is often an unknown underwriter crunching the numbers and making the final decision. Your banker may go to bat for you if the underwriter is questioning certain things, but having your credit cleaned up and documents in order before applying for the loan will make the lending process smoother and faster for everyone.

Check Your Credit Report

The first step in your lending process should be checking and cleaning up your credit report. This is the first item your banker will review. They will use this as a first impression as to your credit worthiness and whether you will be eligible for loans at their institution. The higher your credit score, the more likely you'll be to receive favorable rates as well.

You can check a copy of your credit report for free at annualcreditreport.com. This is the only site that allows truly free copies of your credit report from each of the 3 large reporting agencies, per government regulations. You can keep better tabs on your credit by only pulling from one agency at a time. You are allowed a copy from each agency once a year, so spread out the requests in case something happens in between your reviews.

What Affects Credit Scores

There are 5 major factors that affect your credit score. And sometimes the way the affect your score can seem downright unfair. For instance, credit usage is 30% of your credit score. This is calculated by comparing the amount of credit available to you to the amount of credit you've used. So, owing $900 on a credit card with a $1,000 limit lowers your credit score more than owing $75 on that same credit card. However, you may find that paying off a loan results in lowering your credit score, rather than increasing it. That often happens because the amount of credit available is decreased at the same time that your final amount due reaches $0. One would think that paying off a loan would increase your score as you paid it on time, but the formulas unfortunately don't work that way.

- Payment History - 35%
- Credit Usage - 30%
- Length of Credit History - 15%
- Types of Accounts (credit mix - installment vs revolving) - 10%
- Recent Activity (new credit) - 10%

How Does Your Score Compare?

Below is a summary of the credit score ratings and how much of the population falls within these ranges. If you fall within the very good or excellent ranges, you'll receive the most favorable rates. Falling below those ranges doesn't mean you won't be approved for your loan, you may just have to pay a higher interest rate or jump through a few more hoops before the approval comes through.

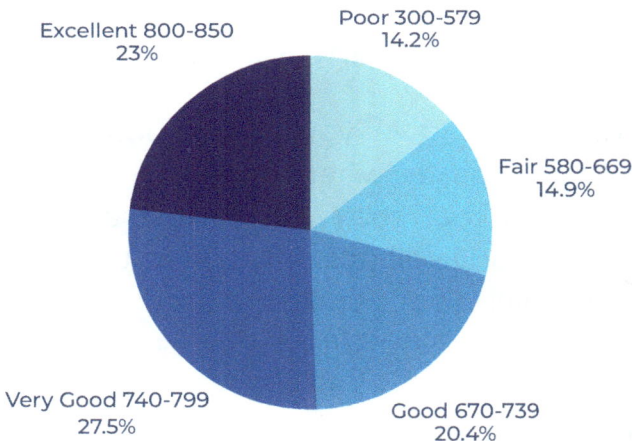

Per Experian Credit Reporting, July 2025

Showing Income in Your Business

Banks will want to see that your business is making money and will be able to make the payments timely now and going into the future. Bankers will often suggest that you show two years' worth of income in the business before applying for any lending. Even then, you may face an uphill battle securing lending as they see self-employed individuals as higher risks and will dig deeper into your financials.

This is a situation where you have to carefully weigh tax savings with lending and outside investor opportunities. It can be tempting to wipe your business income out to zero so you're not paying any tax, but you'll then have a hard time convincing the bank that you have the cash flows to meet your loan obligations. They won't care that there are personal expenses hiding in your tax returns. All tax returns are filed under threat of perjury that the income and taxes are reported accurately, so banks will rely on those documents to verify your historical income.

Gathering Your Documents

Most banks won't give you a comprehensive list of documents to gather when applying for a loan, but there are items that they will almost always ask for. Having these ready will not only speed up the approval process, but will also show the banker that you are organized and handling your finances properly.

For business loans, you'll want to have the following documents ready for review:

- Copy of IRS EIN letter
- Organization documents if you're an LLC
- Partnership agreement, if you're a partnership
- Last three years' business tax returns
- Last three year's personal tax returns
- Current year-to-date balance sheet and income statement
- Details on other loans you have outstanding

Banks also often require owners to co-sign the loan documents and offer some kind of personal guarantee, should the business close or default on the loan. This is especially true if your business doesn't own a lot of assets and has not been open very long.

In this case, you'll also need to provide the banker with personal financial documents.

- Copies of any W2s from jobs outside the business
- Personal financial statement (listing all of your personal assets and liabilities)
- Explanation of any significant increases or decreases in income
- Explanation of any negative items on your credit report

Patience Pays Off

I have received multiple mortgages and bank loans myself and it's never been a stress-free process. I know what will be needed as I complete the application and bankers still find new questions to ask or documentation to ask for.

Lending regulations change regularly, so be patient and try not to take any delays or rejections personally. Ask questions of your banker and take any advice they give to heart. They are just as anxious to lend as you are to receive. They will have feedback you may not have received elsewhere and they can give valuable insight into the current regulatory and lending arena. There are times when the economy is in a downturn and even those with good credit are turned down for new loans. Your banker may also suggest a different lending institution that specializes in your particular needs.

Small Business Administration

The Small Business Administration can be an excellent resource for lending, especially for those just starting their businesses. Their applications are rigorous and can be more frustrating than going with a traditional bank, but they specialize in the needs of self-employed individuals. You may also be able to find grants and educational webinars on their site.

Chapter Eight

Paying Yourself & Your Estimated Taxes

If you are a sole proprietor (or single member LLC), you don't need to run payroll for yourself. In fact, the IRS does not consider sole proprietors to be employees of the business. Your income and expenses are reported on your Schedule C, rather than on a W2.

As your business grows and you begin to have net profits, you can begin to pay yourself. To do this, simply transfer funds from your business bank account to your personal bank account.

This is referred to as an **Owner's Draw**. If you want to know how this affects your financial statements, this would decrease cash in your business bank account, and decrease your owner's equity as you're taking home some of the equity today, rather than taking it home at a later date (such as when you sell the business).

Again, *always keep your business and personal banking transactions separate*. This adds credibility to your finances, as the IRS and lenders won't see personal expenses commingled with the business and wonder which are legitimate. It also protects your LLC if you have one.

An LLC should be treated as a separate, living, breathing entity from you. You wouldn't pay your personal expenses from your brother's bank account. You shouldn't do so from your business's bank account either.

How Much to Pay Yourself

There is no right or wrong answer on how much to pay yourself as you grow, but a good rule of thumb for small businesses in the growth stage is to keep 3 to 6 months' worth of operating expenses on hand. This will give you the cash to cover future expenses during lean months, and to invest in the business as it grows and additional equipment or inventory is needed.

Don't be tempted to get loans to pay yourself. This is the fastest way for a business to go under. A loan can provide temporary cash flow relief, but within a month you'll have to start paying that loan back, plus interest. It can become a dangerous game of robbing Peter to pay Paul and before you know it you're drowning in debt both at home and in the business.

EXAMPLE

Alex started with $5,000 in the bank and has net income of $777. She also has loan payments of $200 she has to make each month.

She would like to pay herself so she can cover expenses at home.

Beginning Cash	$5,000
Net Income	$777
Cash Available	**$5,777**
Operating Expenses/month *(assuming roughly 4x Alex's first week of expenses)*	$800
Cash to Keep in Reserves *(3x Alex's monthly operating expenses)*	**$2,400**

Of the $5,777 in Alex's bank account, she has decided to keep a minimum of $2,400 on hand to cover future operating expenses. She has only made $777 so far from sales. She decides to pay herself $750 after her first week to ensure she has cash on hand to cover future operating expenses or business investment needs.

Estimate Your Owner's Draw (Pay)

You'll need to review the last 12 months' income statements to accurately determine the amount of cash you can take home. If you don't have your financials set up yet, make sure to complete this task so don't inadvertently deplete the business budget and find yourself scrambling to pay bill at the end of the month. The amount you can pay yourself will change as your business grows and matures. The more information you have, the more accurate your calculations will be. Try to average your monthly net income over 12 months so you're including both your slow months and your higher earning months.

Use this table to average out your monthly cash flow needs in the business. Include the figures you're spending on cost of goods sold (COGS), plus all other expenses.

Determine Your Average Monthly Cash Outflows

Month	Loan Pmts	COGS	Expenses	Total
January				
February				
March				
April				
May				
June				
July				
August				
September				
October				
November				
December				
Totals				
Average (Divide by 12)				

Determine Your Cash Reserves

Average Loan Pmts

_____

Average COGS

_____

Average Expenses

_____

Total Monthly Cash Needed

_____

Months of Cash Reserves Needed
(3 to 6 months is suggested)

_____

Total Cash to Keep in Bank
(Cash Needed x Months in Reserves)

_____

When you are paying yourself, make sure it does not drain the cash in your bank below the "Total Cash to Keep in Bank" figure above. It may be tempting to take out extra cash for holiday gifts or summer vacation, but you may then find yourself scrambling for cash in the business several months later.

Now let's calculate the average monthly net income generated by your business to determine how much your business is able to pay you on a monthly basis.

Determine Your Average Net Income

Month	Gross Sales	Less COGS	Less Expenses	Net Income
January				
February				
March				
April				
May				
June				
July				
August				
September				
October				
November				
December				
Totals				
Average (Divide by 12)				

Use your average monthly net income as a guidepost in determining your take-home pay. If you have enough cash in the bank to comfortably cover future overhead expenses and loan payments, then you can take home your average monthly earnings (or even a little more if you want to recoup your initial investment). If your cash reserves are less than what is needed to keep the business afloat during lean times, then you may need to take a smaller pay in the beginning until sales increase.

Use this worksheet as a guide and tweak your estimates often as your business grows. Every business is different, and risk tolerances vary. Use it as a reminder to keep both business and personal budgets in mind when paying yourself throughout the year.

Calculating Your Estimated Taxes

Taxes are complicated, as every tax return is different. The tax due to the IRS at the end of the year is a culmination of taxes due on wages from other jobs (yours and/or your spouse's), investment income, retirement earnings, rental property activity, allowed deductions, and various tax credits.

Owning a business adds yet another layer of complexity to this calculation as you need to pay in not only your federal taxes, but also your FICA (Social Security & Medicare) taxes with your Form 1040 at the end of the year.

If there is one thing that shocks clients when they open a business and get their tax return that first year, it's the self-employment taxes. They may have received refunds in prior years, but now I'm telling them they owe $7,000 with their tax return. How did that happen?!

When you're an employee, you not only have federal taxes taken out of your paycheck, but the Social Security and Medicare taxes are withheld as well. And those tend to be out-of-sight, out-of-mind. Employees typically have no idea how much they're truly paying in taxes because they focus on the net pay and don't review the paystubs often, if ever. On top of that, your employer is matching your Social Security and Medicare contributions, so you're only on the hook for half of the total taxes paid into the system.

When you become self-employed, you wear both employer and employee hats, so you have to pay in both halves of the FICA taxes. And to add insult to injury, there's no paycheck to withhold those from, so they become another line item and tax due with your Form 1040 at the end of the year. Where employees are blissfully ignorant of the total tax picture, your 1040 throws that amount in your face every year.

Like any other business, the government has bills to pay and they don't take kindly to being paid on the net-365 method. We'd all like to just keep the money and send one big check to the IRS at the end of the year, but Congress has created rules to ensure everyone pays in their taxes regularly, via either paycheck withholdings or estimated tax payments.

If you don't pay in estimates on a regular basis, you'll be hit with interest and penalties on top of the tax you already owe. To set a floor on how much needs to be paid in to avoid penalties, you must pay in 100% of the prior year's tax, or 90% of the current year's tax, via withholdings or quarterly estimates in order to avoid penalties.

The IRS doesn't care how they receive the money, as long as they receive it regularly and timely. If you don't think you're disciplined enough to calculate and pay in your quarterly estimates, and you have another W2 job, or your spouse works, increase the withholdings from one of those paychecks. All of your payments (withholdings, estimates, and overpayments from a prior year) are ultimately added together on your 1040 to determine the balance you owe the IRS by April 15.

If math isn't your forte, this is where investing in professional tax guidance pays for itself. It's usually cheaper (and less stressful) than receiving IRS penalty notices.

Calculating Your Estimated Taxes

There are several ways to review your income and calculate the estimates you should pay in for the prior year. They range in complication and accuracy, so tread carefully and engage the help of a professional if you have a more complicated tax return. Option #1 pays in the bare minimum to avoid penalties for underpayment (and could still result in a big tax bill at the end of the year). Option #2 gets you a more accurate figure to avoid any surprises at the end of the year, but involves reviewing your year-to-date financials and running a projected tax return mid-year.

Option #1 - Cover 100% of Prior Year's Tax

This method simply keeps you on the right side of the IRS to avoid penalties for underpaying your taxes, based on the prior year's tax figure. This does not take into account your current year taxable income. You could still owe a big liability when your tax return is filed, or you could have a refund coming to you. But at least you won't be a deadbeat taxpayer in the eyes of the IRS.

You'll need to look at your prior year's tax return to calculate your estimates via this method. You need to pay in at least the amount of total tax calculated on your 1040 from the prior year.

Total Tax on Line 24 of your 2024 1040

_____

Less: Anticipated withholdings
from wages or retirement in
current year

_____

**Difference to cover via
quarterly estimates or
additional withholdings**

_____

Note: *You're not covering the balance due on your tax return at the bottom of page 2 from the prior year. That figure simply shows whether you paid in too much (you received a refund) or too little (you owe the IRS a balance) the prior year. This doesn't indicate the total tax that you paid on your various sources of income.*

Option #2 - Paying Quarterly Taxes on Business Income

This method takes into account your net income each quarter and multiplies it by your anticipated tax rate and self-employment taxes to ensure your estimates cover taxes generated by your business income.

Start by looking at your prior year's effective tax rate on your tax return. *(If you have significant changes in your income situation, keep in mind that this could go up or down each year.)*

A) Tax on Line 16 of your 2024
Form 1040

_____

B) Taxable Income on Line 15 of your
2024 Form 1040

/ _____

C) Effective Tax Rate (A divided by B)   =
_____

Next, calculate your net business income each quarter by the following figures to get your quarterly estimates. This is a VERY rough estimate and isn't guaranteed to keep you from owing the IRS penalties/interest. This is not recommended if you don't have a good handle on your taxable income and allowed business expenses. If done properly, this can help you control cash flows and avoid a big amount due or overpaid at the end of the year.

Quarterly Net Income x Effective Tax Rate

PLUS

Quarterly Net Income x FICA taxes (15.3%)

Quarterly Net Income

_____

Effective Tax Rate (calculated above)   X
_____

Federal tax due for quarter   =
_____

PLUS

Quarterly Net Income

_____

Self-Employment Tax (15.3%)   X _____ .153

Self-Employment tax due for quarter = _____

Quarterly Estimates

Quarter 1 (January thru March)
Due April 15   _____

Quarter 2 (April thru May)
Due June 15   _____

Quarter 3 (June through August)
Due September 15   _____

Quarter 4 (September thru December)
Due January 15   _____

Option #3 - Hiring a Professional

The best way to stay on top of your quarterly income and estimates is to review your figures quarterly with a qualified professional. They can do a tax projection which takes into account your anticipated income from all sources during the year, including your YTD business income. A tax projection involves creating an estimate of your tax return at various times throughout the year to determine how current tax laws and tax rates coincide with your current income, withholdings, and estimates.

When done properly, these projections not only save you the stress of underpaying your taxes throughout the year, but they can provide options for tax saving conversations before year-end.

Please keep in mind that this is a gross oversimplification of a tax return. I showed just enough to introduce estimated tax options. If I went through all of the pieces of your tax return, you would understand why schools don't teach tax preparation to students. Most parents would be begging for the days when Common Core math was the bane of their existence.

Taxes Based on Net Income - Not Owner Draws

Note that none of the tax calculations took into account Alex's take-home pay (her owner draws). **The IRS wants their tax on everything you earned as of December 31 each year, even if you left it in the business to cover operating expenses or future growth needs, or used it to pay down loans.** The IRS doesn't care when you pay yourself, only when the income was earned. But this also means your owner draws aren't taxed later when you take them, so don't worry about being double-taxed. Once you pay tax on your business earnings, those funds are yours to take home as cash flows allow.

Here are Alex's options for paying in estimated taxes for the current tax year. She's young and lives the simple life, so no spouse, no dependents, and no other jobs or income to account for.

Option #1 - Cover 100% of Prior Year's Tax

Alex looks at her prior year tax return. Her tax on line 24 was $8,000. If she takes the simple route, she would pay in ¼ of that ($2,000) as payments on April 15, June 15, September 15, and January 15 to avoid IRS penalties & interest.

Option #2 - Paying Quarterly Taxes on Business Income

Alex decides to try her hand at calculating her estimates based on her first 3 months' income. She made $1,800 in month 1; $2,345 in month 2; and $2,680 in month 3. Her total business income is $6,825. Her prior year effective tax rate was 12%.

She calculates her estimates as follows:

Federal Tax - $6,825 x 12% = $819
Social Security & Medicare Tax - $6,825 x 15.3% = $1,044

Total estimate due to the IRS for this quarter would be $1,863

Chapter Nine

Paying Yourself as an S-Corp Shareholder

If your business grows to the point where being taxed as an S-Corporation makes sense, then you will need to place yourself on payroll as you are now both a shareholder and an employee within the business. You will be wearing two hats from a tax perspective, so you will receive two forms to report your income to the IRS. A W-2 to report your salary and a K-1 to report the income you earned as a shareholder.

An S-Corporation can be an effective way to save taxes as earnings above and beyond reasonable compensation for owners is not subject to self-employment taxes. That can result in significant tax savings.

However, the IRS requires that S-Corporation owners take a reasonable salary for work they perform within the business. Ask yourself what you would pay an unrelated third party, with the same skillset, to perform the same duties you do on a daily basis. This should be the compensation you report on a W-2.

Those W-2 earnings are subject to Federal, Social Security, Medicare, and any state and local taxes. Just as they are for other employees.

As we discussed in the previous chapter, as a sole proprietor you pay yourself with distributions and pay taxes via estimated tax payments to the IRS.

| Owner | → | **Taxable Income** | → | **Estimated Taxes** |
| | | *Subject to Federal, SS, MC, State* | | *Paid Quarterly* |

*Pay yourself distributions as income & cash flows allow - Tax is calculated on Taxable Income, **not distributions** taken during the year*

Owner-shareholders are paid both a reasonable salary in an S-Corporation and distributions on other earnings throughout the year if the business is profitable and cash flows allow. Any business net income above and beyond their W-2 earnings are reported on a Form K-1 and are taxed as investment earnings on the shareholder's Form 1040. No taxes are withheld from these distributions, so estimated tax payments must be made on these earnings to avoid IRS penalties at the end of the year.

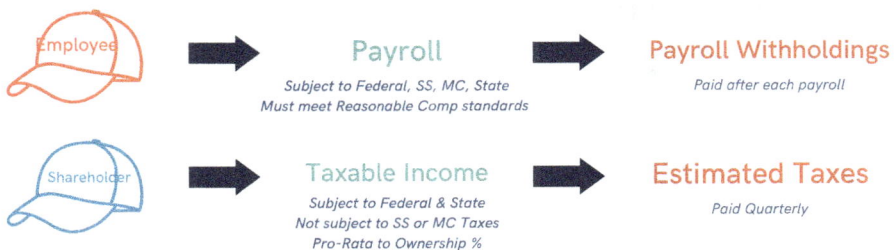

Employee	→	**Payroll**	→	**Payroll Withholdings**
		Subject to Federal, SS, MC, State		*Paid after each payroll*
		Must meet Reasonable Comp standards		
Shareholder	→	**Taxable Income**	→	**Estimated Taxes**
		Subject to Federal & State		*Paid Quarterly*
		Not subject to SS or MC Taxes		
		Pro-Rata to Ownership %		

As an employee of the corporation, you may participate in any employer-sponsored 401k plans, just as other employees would. You can make pre-tax contributions, as well as enjoying the benefits of employer-matched contributions, which are deductible as a business expense. You could also choose to contribute to a SEP plan or simply make personal IRA contributions. I encourage you to consult with both a financial advisor and CPA to find the best solution that allows you to meet your savings goals and save the most in tax at the end of the year.

S-Corporation Health Insurance

Health insurance premiums for a shareholder that owns more than 2% of stock in an S-Corporation is treated differently than that of other employees. Any premiums that the business pays on behalf of you and your family must be included in Box 1 of your W2 so it is reported on your Form 1040 as taxable income.

You then deduct this amount as self-employed health insurance on your Form 1040, just as you would as a sole proprietor or partner in a partnership. It's a lot of hoops to jump through to get a tax deduction. It's a process that made more sense many years ago under old tax rules. Congress and the IRS just never bothered to update tax procedures to simplify things.

Because these procedures are still required under the current tax code, an agent could disallow this health insurance deduction if it's isn't reported on the W2 and deducted on the Form 1040 correctly. This is an important area to get right when setting yourself up on payroll. Most onlline payroll processors, such as Gusto, make this easy to incorporate into year-end reporting though.

Let's look at an example of a simple S-Corporation payroll situation to put all of this information together. It can be confusing in the beginning, so this may be a moment when you want to reach out for professional guidance to get it all correct.

- Living the Dream LLC has elected to be taxed as an S-Corporation
- The entity has 2 active owners
  - John is CEO with 51% ownership
  - Paul is the Operations Manager with 49% ownership
- Reasonable Salaries based on industry standard for their roles within the company
  - John is paid $75,000
  - Paul is paid $60,000
- Health insurance is paid by the company for John, but Paul has health insurance through his spouse's employer
  - John's health insurance is $500/month
- The company grossed $450,000 and had expenses of $350,000 for the year (including the owners' payroll and John's health insurance) for Taxable Income of $100,000
- The owners have decided to leave $40,000 in the bank to cover ongoing expenses. They agree to distribute the remaining $60,000 in earnings to the shareholders.

- John receives $30,600 in distributions (51% of $60,000)
- Paul receives $29,400 in distributions (49% of $60,000)
- They must each pay estimated taxes on their share of the $100,000 in Taxable Income on their individual returns
  - John's estimates are calculated on $51,000 (51% of $100,000)
  - Paul's estimates are calculated on $49,000 (49% $100,000)

John's Figures - 51% Shareholder

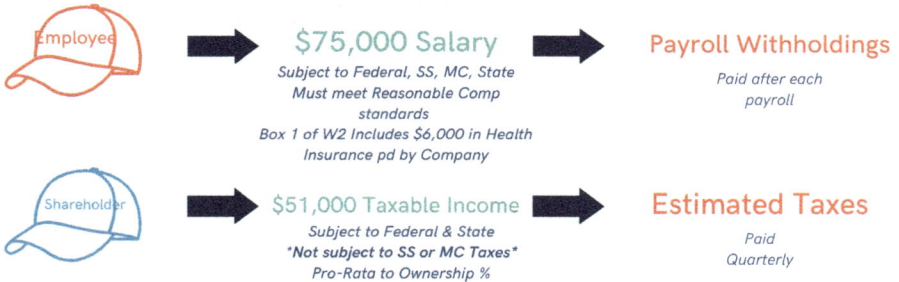

Employee → **$75,000 Salary**
Subject to Federal, SS, MC, State
Must meet Reasonable Comp standards
Box 1 of W2 Includes $6,000 in Health Insurance pd by Company
→ **Payroll Withholdings**
Paid after each payroll

Shareholder → $51,000 Taxable Income
Subject to Federal & State
"Not subject to SS or MC Taxes"
Pro-Rata to Ownership %
→ **Estimated Taxes**
Paid Quarterly

John receives cash distributions of $30,600 (51% of $60,000 in distrubutions paid)

Paul's Figures - 49% Shareholder

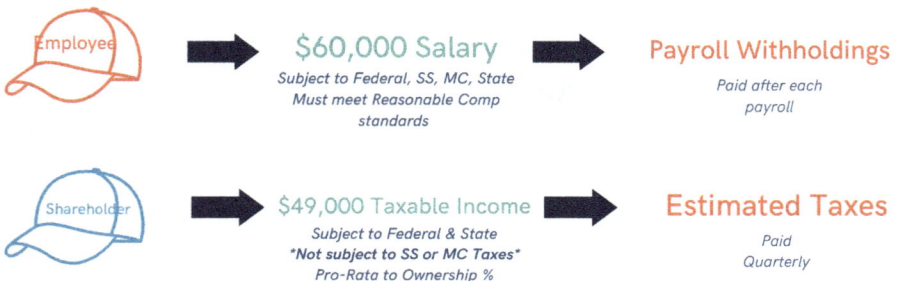

Employee → **$60,000 Salary**
Subject to Federal, SS, MC, State
Must meet Reasonable Comp standards
→ **Payroll Withholdings**
Paid after each payroll

Shareholder → $49,000 Taxable Income
Subject to Federal & State
"Not subject to SS or MC Taxes"
Pro-Rata to Ownership %
→ **Estimated Taxes**
Paid Quarterly

Paul receives cash distributions of $29,400 (49% of $60,000 in distrubutions paid)

Other S-Corporation Matters

I have not gone through all of the intricacies related to S-Corporations because shareholder basis and other complicated tax matters are beyond the scope of this book. I wanted to make sure you had a basic understanding of S-Corporation payroll, in case you are pondering that tax election.

There are a couple of other matters to keep in mind if you decide to elect to become an S-Corporation.

Distributions are not as flexible as they are in partnerships. In a partnership, you can make changes in partner distribution percentages by simply changing your partnership agreement. This is helpful is one partner starts taking on a larger share of the duties. In an S-Corporation, all distributions of earnings must be made according to a shareholder's ownership percentage. So, if you have 2 owners with a 60/40 split in ownership, you would give the 60% owner $600 and the 40% owner $400 of a $1,000 cash distribution. This is because shareholders own stock in an S-Corporation and stock shares would have to be bought/sold in order to change the ownership and income split percentages.

Also, be sure to hold shareholder meetings at least once a year and keep meeting minutes. These don't have to be complex, just note the date and time the shareholders met and any business topics or decisions addressed. This ensures that you are truly behaving as a corporation and keeps the IRS from revoking your S-Corporation election.

Annual S-Corporation Compliance Checklist

☐ **Confirm shareholders are receiving "reasonable" compensation**
Ensure active shareholders are receiving "reasonable" compensation for services rendered to the corporation

☐ **Understand tax rules of shareholder distributions in a year the business is showing a loss**
If the business is showing a loss, confirm that shareholders are not taking distributions in excess of their basis in the corporation. (Excess distributions are subject to specific taxation rules on the shareholder's individual return.)

☐ **Include health insurance premiums >2% shareholders in their W-2**
Health insurance premiums for more than 2% shareholders must be paid for by the corporation, or reimbursed to the shareholder by the corporation, and included in the shareholder's W-2. (The shareholder is allowed an above-the-line deduction for these premiums on their Form 1040.)

☐ **Don't commingle funds**
Shareholders own stock in the business, much as you would buy stock in a publicly traded corporation. The corporation should not pay personal expenses for employees or shareholders without being reimbursed or having a loan document in place with specific repayment terms.

☐ **Make distributions in proportion to each shareholder's ownership percentage**
Distributions from a corporation are seen as dividend distributions by the IRS, which is why they are not subject to FICA taxes. S-Corps are only allowed to have one type of stock, so all distributions must be made to shareholders in the same manner and in amounts equal to their ownership percentage at the time of the distribution. (If you have two shareholders each owning 50% of the stock, just ensure that each owner receives $500 if you're distributing $1,000.)

☐ **Review whether your state requires annual meeting minutes to be created for LLCs and S-Corps**
Have proper legal documents in place for any related-party transactions.

Chapter Ten

Business Deductions - Save Taxes Like a Pro

One of the most frequent questions I field from small business clients is "What expenses can I deduct"? The tax code regarding business deductions is complex with exceptions to every rule, but there are some basic guidelines that you can use when determining whether something is a deductible business expense and whether it would pass the scrutiny of a tax auditor. This chapter will outline the IRS definition of deductible business expenses and give some common examples.

When planning your budget for the year or making decisions on whether to move forward with a specific business expenditure (especially if it's a large purchase), engage your accountant in the decision-making process if the expense seems unusual and you're unsure if it's tax deductible. They can best advise you on the possible tax savings in your particular situation, especially considering the fact that each state has its own tax code, which often differs from Federal tax laws. The tax savings (or lack thereof) may sway your decision on whether or not to ultimately make the purchase.

One thing to keep in mind is that just because an expense isn't tax deductible doesn't mean you're prohibited from spending the business funds on a particular item. It's completely up to you, as the business owner, to decide how best to build the business and your brand. You may just have to forego the tax savings on certain expenditures.

Client entertainment is a perfect example of this. I'll discuss this particular item in more detail later on in this chapter, but it's often an expense that business owners find well worth the cost as it can bring a large return on the investment, despite the fact that the tax code now disallows these expenses as tax deductions.

Ordinary & Necessary

The IRS allows deductions for expenses that are deemed to be ordinary and necessary for a particular business. It defines ordinary as those expenses that are "common and accepted" in the course of a particular industry. Necessary expenses are those that are "helpful and appropriate" according to the tax code. Some expenses, such as advertising and postage, are common across most industries, while others, such as shampoo and hairdryers are not necessary for a bookkeeping firm, but most definitely are for salons.

An **ordinary** expense is one that is common and accepted in your industry

> A **necessary** expense is one that is helpful and appropriate for your trade or business.

There are some gray areas that even leave professional tax preparers stumped and referring to court cases and tax laws to determine their deductibility. One such area is expenses that social media influencers incur in their business. Can the wardrobe, makeup artist, pedicure, or being on-site at that luxury beach for the photo shoot be deducted? These are situations where the answer may legitimately be "it depends", so set up some time for an in-depth conversation with your accountant before assuming these items will show up on your tax return as deductible expenses.

Make Decisions Based on Growth, Not Taxes

Even if an expense is tax deductible, there may be limitations on how much can be deducted each year, such as with business meals and depreciable fixed assets. Many small business owners stress about the amount of taxes that will be due at the end of a profitable year and are tempted to spend as much as possible before December 31 to alleviate their tax liability for the year. Rather than spending down cash that may be put to better use in the next year, stay focused on the long-term health and growth of the business.

A good rule of thumb is to spend money on things that are important to the business and will move it forward a positive financial direction. If you need a piece of equipment at the end of the year, then by all means make the purchase by December 31 to decrease your tax burden. But don't purchase it solely to save taxes. You should engage your accountant to do tax planning before making that large purchase. You may be surprised to find that you're spending $20,000 to save $3,000, depending on your tax bracket and the business entity structure.

You may also decide that foregoing a tax deduction is the best course of action. If you spend $500 on entertaining a potential client for the evening, you may find that missing out on $100 or so in tax savings is more than worth the thousands of dollars in future business this client could bring in.

You should also consider that your business may be better served by keeping that money invested for a rainy day. Banks and other lenders make decisions based on financial statements and tax returns, and they look 2-3 years back to see if the business has had healthy cash flows which will allow it to meet the requested loan obligations. They don't tend to lend money to a business that consistently shows little or no income, especially if it has few assets that the bank can attach as collateral.

If you have exhausted all the tax savings opportunities available to you without draining your bank account, you may have to accept the tax bill as a cost of doing business, much as interest paid on loans. Taxes can be a bitter pill to swallow, but it's better to have a healthy and thriving business than to have losses year after year and wondering how long you will have a viable entity.

Common Business Deductions

There are some business deductions that are common to many industries. They are so standard that the IRS specifically lists these on business returns. As long as you can show proof of payment of these expenses and they meet the "ordinary and necessary" test for your particular business, you should feel fairly confident in deducting these common expenses. This list is by no means all-inclusive, but it will give you an idea of what other businesses are deducting and what the IRS allows.

- Advertising
- Auto
- Commission & fees
- Contract Labor
- Depreciation
- Dues & licenses
- Employee benefit programs
- Insurance
- Interest
- Legal & professional fees
- Meals
- Office supplies
- Postage
- Rent (real estate or equipment)
- Repairs & maintenance
- Supplies
- Taxes

- Telephone
- Travel
- Uniforms (only clothing not suitable for street wear)
- Utilities
- Wages

Non-Deductible Expenses

The expenses below are examples of expenditures that are non-deductible, even if you feel they serve a legitimate business purpose. (Remember that this doesn't mean you can't have these business expenses, it just means you can't deduct them on your tax return.) Keep your business deductions reasonable as well, as unusual or extraordinarily high expenses can trigger the IRS computers to flag your return for an audit or review. The IRS does compare business expenses across industries of the same type and size to determine if expenses may need further review. If you have more travel expenses than others in your industry, or if all of your expenses are rounded off to the nearest hundred dollars, that can increase your chances of being audited, so keep things reasonable and well-documented.

- Clothing that is suitable for street wear & related dry cleaning
- Fines & penalties
- Meals without a specific business purpose
- Officer life insurance premiums
- Personal expenses
- Principal payments on loans
- Taxes paid for individual income tax liabilities (including estimated tax payments)

Depreciation

Depreciation is the reduction in value of an asset over time, due to wear and tear. Depreciation rules are complex and vary greatly based on the type of asset being purchased. A couple of important concepts will be discussed here, for educational purposes. Your tax preparer will prepare depreciation schedules when preparing your tax return and financial statements. This is an important schedule to keep, as the depreciation taken (or allowed if a taxpayer failed to take the proper amount) is taken into consideration when calculating any gains or losses when selling or disposing of assets.

For cash flow purposes, your depreciation deduction may not match the cash you paid for an asset in a particular tax year. If you purchase a building for $500,000 you won't get to write off the entire $500,000 in the year of purchase. For commercial buildings, you deduct the cost of the building over 39 years for tax purposes. If it is a residential rental, then you will deduct the cost over 27.5 years. If you're taking out a loan for the purchase, then you may not feel the negative effects of this deduction limitation too harshly. However, if you're using cash from the business to make the purchase, you may feel the pinch of draining your cash reserves while also paying more taxes than you had anticipated. If interest rates are reasonable, using bank money to allow you to keep cash in the business to cover taxes and other operating expenses may be a better long-term budgeting strategy.

Improvements vs Repairs

The tax code lays out the rules for determining whether certain expenditures are repairs that can be written off as they're incurred, or improvements, which must be depreciated based on the type of asset and its expected useful life. Facts and circumstances need to be reviewed in detail to make a specific determination based on current tax laws. Be sure to keep written receipts and detailed documentation on all fixed asset and repair expenditures. Your accountant will need to understand these details in order to handle these items properly on your depreciation schedule each year.

Improvements (Depreciate)

Taxpayer A finds that the roof on their pizza shop is beyond repair and needs to be fully replaced. The total cost of this replacement is $15,000. Although the taxpayer completes and pays for this replacement by December 31 of the current tax year, they do not get the full $15,000 deduction on their tax return. Because this new roof extended the life of a commercial building, the IRS requires that this expense be depreciated over 39 years. In this case, the taxpayer will get a deduction of roughly $385 for each of the next 39 years.

vs

Repairs (Expense)

Taxpayer B finds that the roof on their salon was damaged in a recent storm. The damage is isolated to one section of the roof and can be repaired without replacing the entire roof. The cost to repair the roof is $2,500. Because this is a repair and the bulk of the existing roof was left intact, this can be fully written off as long as the work is done and the payment is made by the close of the tax year.

Section 179 Deduction

You may have had vendors reach out to you regarding equipment purchases near the end of the year with information stating that you can deduct 100% of the purchase price of the equipment, thus reaping substantial tax savings. Although this may be true, like all tax laws, there are limitations to these deductions and you should speak with your tax advisor before making any large purchases.

First of all, you cannot take Section 179 expenses if they will put you into a loss, so if you don't have a significant tax liability at the end of the year, it may not be the year to make that large purchase. There are carryforward rules for unused Section 179 expenses, but that discussion is best left to your tax planning meeting with your CPA prior to year-end. This and other reasons that will be noted within this book underscore the need for all business owners to keep current and accurate financial records, regardless of their size.

Also, some items, such as certain vehicles, may not be eligible for Section 179 deductions. The IRS puts limitations on vehicle gross weights and business use percentages to determine if it is appropriate to fully deduct these items in one year. Passenger vehicles are limited in their deductibility as the IRS assumes that they are also used for personal purposes, unless it is clear that the vehicle has been specifically outfitted for business-use only (such as ambulances or cargo vans).

Meals & Entertainment

Deductible Meals

Business meals are another popular deduction, but also one with multiple IRS restrictions and heavy scrutiny. **In order for meals to be deducted, they must have a business purpose and be documented.** Even then, they are limited to 50% of the cost of the meal. When deducting business meals, make sure that you keep receipts and note with whom you met and the business purpose of the meeting. The IRS will request this documentation if your return is ever chosen for examination. Because business meals are limited to a 50% deduction, many business owners are surprised by the limited tax savings these produce. If you spend $1,000 in business meals during the year, you are limited to a $500 deduction on your tax return. If you are in the 22% tax bracket, this results in a tax savings of $110 (not taking into account any self-employment taxes). The tax savings would be even less for those in a lower tax bracket. Although every dollar counts, this is an easy area for an agent to scrutinize and you may be taking a risky position for minimal tax savings.

Meals provided to and for employees are treated differently and may be 100% deductible, under certain circumstances. If the meals are for the convenience of the employer (such as working overtime) and provided to the employees on the employer's premises, then it is fully deductible. You can also fully deduct meals provided to employees off-premises if they are for events such as picnics and holiday parties. Reimbursed meals for employees traveling on business are generally limited to the 50% deduction, however, just as they would be for the business owner.

Non-Deductible Meals & Entertainment

In addition to disallowing meals that aren't properly documented, the IRS also disallows any meals purchased during work hours that don't have a specific work purpose. So, don't bother trying to deduct that latte you purchased on the way to the office or that burger you grabbed on the way to a client's office across town. Those are both non-deductible purchases.

The Taxpayer Cuts and Jobs Act of 2017 made some major changes to the entertainment portion of the tax code and made **all entertainment related expenses non-deductible**. Tickets to sporting and theater events are no longer tax deductible. In order to deduct the meals purchased at the event, the food and drinks must be purchased separately from the event itself. If you are paying for everything on one bill, make sure that the cost of the event is listed separately from the food purchased so it's clear what was deducted on the tax return.

100% Deductible

- Company-wide party
- Meals provided to employees working overtime on employer's premises
- Meals & entertainment included in employee compensation
- Food & drink provided free of charge to the public

- Documented meals with a client
- Meals out of the office with staff
- Office snacks and meals
- Employee meals while traveling or while attending a conference
- Food purchased for board meetings

50% Deductible*

Several of these items were made 100% deductible for the 2021 & 2022 tax years, due to the pandemic in order to help restaurants get back on their feet.

Vehicle Deductions

Taking a deduction for a business vehicle, or business-use of your personal vehicle is super easy in two respects. First of all, it's as easy as tracking mileage to get a deduction on your tax return. On the other hand, it's even easier to lose the deduction (and owe back taxes plus penalties and interest) if you don't have proper documentation to back up the mileage.

There is often confusion on which miles can be deducted and how to handle things if you're using a vehicle for both business and personal travel. I'll walk you through the simplest ways to receive the deductions you deserve, but also how to document your expenses so the IRS doesn't remove those from your tax return with the stroke of a pen.

Tracking Mileage

The key to protecting any business deductions (pardon the pun) is to document your mileage and any expenses for repairs, fuel, car washes, or insurance. Tracking your mileage is imperative if you're using a vehicle for business purposes, whether you're taking the standard deduction, or taking actual expenses.

You can choose to go old-school in tracking your mileage by writing down your beginning and ending mileage and other pertinent details for each business trip. You can keep a pad of paper in your car, use an electronic notepad in your phone, or buy a mileage logbook at an office supply store. Just make sure the trip details you track include trip beginning mileage, the business purpose of the trip, and ending mileage on your vehicle.

If you aren't one to remember to write down all those details every time you start your car, you may want to consider utilizing an app such as MileIQ to automatically track your mileage. Mileage apps allow you to indicate whether a trip is business or personal and you can note the business purpose right right in your phone. At the end of the year, the app will provide a report that you can use for tax reporting purposes.

Deductible vs Non-Deductible Miles

Not all miles that you drive during the work day are considered business-purpose or deductible. You need to have a specific business purpose for the trip in order for the IRS to allow the deduction. The one area that trips a lot of people up is commuting back and forth to the office or your store. **These trips are considered commuting miles and are not deductible**, even though they do feel like business miles to you. This is where many social media posts and business owners share the theory that if you have a business (aka LLC magic wand), then you can deduct your vehicle in full. This just isn't true, unfortunately.

Your business is allowed vehicle deductions, but it can't write off all the lease payments on your new BMW when you're using the vehicle to go to the office, occasionally meet with clients, and then take the kiddos to soccer practice after work. Sorry to be the bearer of bad news!

Deductible Miles

✓ Meeting with client at their place of business

✓ Meeting with professionals for business-related meetings (accountant, attorney, banker, other consultants)

✓ Lunch with client or other third party for business purposes

✓ Running business errands such as going to the bank, post office, or office supply store

✓ Travel to airport or out-of-town destination for business meeting or conference

✓ Travel between office/primary business locations

Non-Deductible Miles

✗ Driving to/from the office/primary business location (this is considered commuting)

✗ Grabbing lunch or running other personal errands during the work day

✗ Unsubstantiated trips (no mileage log kept)

✗ Personal miles driven in a vehicle owned by the business

Mileage Deductibility Example

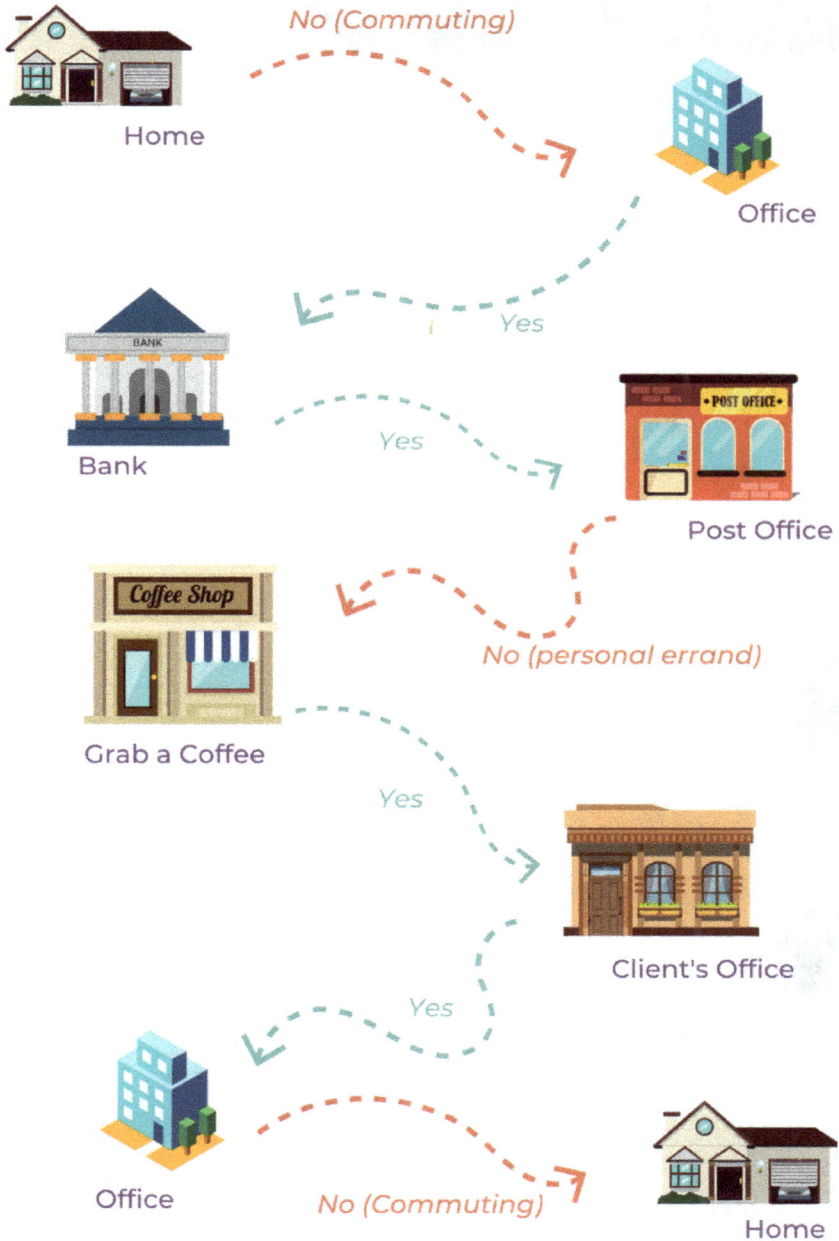

Home

No (Commuting)

Office

Yes

Bank

Yes

Post Office

No (personal errand)

Grab a Coffee

Yes

Client's Office

Yes

Office

No (Commuting)

Home

Mileage Tracker

Month	Business Miles	Commuting Miles	Personal Miles	Total Miles
January				
February				
March				
April				
May				
June				
July				
August				
September				
October				
November				
December				
TOTALS				

Utilizing the Standard Mileage Rate

Miles Driven for Business Purposes	
Miles Driven for Commuting Purposes	
Miles Driven for Personal Purposes	
Total Mileage on Vehicle For the Year	
Mileage Deduction (Business Miles x .70) *2025 IRS Rate*	
Total Parking Expenses (Business Purpose)	
Total Tolls (Business Purpose)	

Parking and tolls related to business travel are 100% deductible as a business expense, regardless of the number of business miles driven during the year.

You must use the standard mileage rate in the first year you use a vehicle for business purposes in order to have the option of deciding between mileage or actual expenses in later years.

Utilizing the Actual Expense Deduction

Repairs & Maintenance	
Car Washes	
Gas	
Registration Fees	
Licenses	
Depreciation	
Interest on Loan	
Lease Payments	
Miles Driven for Business Purposes	
Miles Driven for Commuting Purposes	
Miles Driven for Personal Purposes	
Total Mileage on Vehicle For the Tax Year	

Personal Expenses

There are some personal expenses that can be written off on your tax return. Some of these are written off directly on your Schedule C and will save you self-employment taxes. Others have to be reported on other schedules on your tax return and will save you federal tax, but won't reduce your business income to save self-employment taxes (such as self-employed health insurance and IRA contributions).

Below are a list of items to include on your tax return to reduce your tax liability as much as possible:

- **Personal use of cell phone** - Direct deduction on Schedule C. Prorate your bill between business and personal use as the IRS won't believe you are using it 100% for business unless you have 2 separate phones you're using. Exclude the portion of the bill allocated to family members' phones.
- **Home Internet** - If you are working from home, you can prorate part of your home internet service. Again, prorate this between personal and business use. This is also a direct deduction on your Schedule C and will save both federal & self-employment tax.
- **Health Insurance** - Your family health insurance premiums are reported on a separate schedule on your Form 1040 and won't reduce self-employment tax, but they will reduce your federal tax liability.
- **IRA Contributions** - If cash flows allow, you can also deduct any traditional IRA contributions you make (subject to income limitations). If you contribute to a Roth IRA, the contributions are deductible, but withdrawals aren't taxable.

Chapter Eleven

Home Office Deduction - No Audit Ahead

An often missed and misunderstood deduction for small businesses is the home office deduction. Many small business owners believe that taking this deduction will increase your chances of being audited. This isn't the case at all. The IRS encourages taxpayers to take all deductions and credits they're eligible for. In fact, if you're audited, the IRS will actually adjust a return in your favor if they find that legitimate deductions were missed and deadlines have not passed. I know, hard to believe, right?

Not only is the home office deduction allowed, and encouraged, but a simplified method has been created, which is based solely on the square footage of your office and does not require any utility or other expense receipts. Small business owners find themselves on the wrong side of the IRS when they deduct a space that does not meet the definition of a home office, or they overestimate the size of the office. As long as you have documentation and follow the rules, this is a simple deduction to take each year.

Definition of Home Office

The IRS defines a home office as one that is used **regularly** and **exclusively** for business purposes. If you have a storage shed you're using to store inventory, or a spare bedroom you've converted into an office, those would typically meet the definition of a home office.

Your home office should be your principal place of business. Use of additional space outside of your home doesn't specifically preclude you from take the deduction, as long as your home office is used substantially and regularly.

If your office space is used in one of the following ways, it will typically qualify as a space that is used **regularly** for business purposes:

- As your principal place of business for your trade or business;
- As a place where you meet or deal with your patients, clients, or customers in the normal course of your trade or business;
- A separate structure that's not attached to your home, and is used exclusively on a regular basis in connection with your trade or business;
- On a regular basis for storage of inventory or product samples used in your trade or business of selling products at retail or wholesale, so long as your home is the sole fixed location of such trade or business;
- For rental use; or
- As a daycare facility.

The space must also be used exclusively for business purposes. Doing occasional paperwork in your dining room won't make the room eligible for a home office deduction. Another common scenario is use of a spare bedroom for both business and personal purposes. If the room is mixed-use, create a barrier that separates the office space from the rest of the room and prorate the square footage accordingly.

If you are unsure about the deduction, put yourself in an IRS agent's shoes. If you were the agent looking over the space, would it obviously be a home office, or would there be some question as to its intended purpose? This is a helpful deduction, but it rarely makes or breaks a tax return, so don't give an agent reason to question other deductions on your return because your home office was actually where your kids spent their evenings playing video games.

Below are some helpful questions to ask yourself when determining if a space meets the IRS guidelines:

- If an agent requested to see your home office space, will they agree that it's used exclusively for business purposes?
- Does it look like an office you'd have off-site?
- If using a separate space, is it used exclusively for inventory? Or are you parking your car & storing personal items there as well?
- If using a spare bedroom, is there a bed and dresser in there for guest use?
- If a room is mixed-use, do you have the business space separated by a screen or other divider?

Calculating the Deduction

There are two methods to use when calculating your home office deduction. The first is the Simplified (safe harbor) method, which requires no receipts or documentation. The second method, Regular (long calculation), may lead to a larger deduction, but requires that receipts for utilities, repairs, and other expenses to the space being gathered and summarized.

Simplified Method (Safe Harbor)

This method works in a very similar manner to taking mileage on your personal vehicle. You simply multiply the square footage of your home office by a fixed amount set by the tax code for the year. The tax code currently allows for $5 per square foot of your home office. As I noted above, there is no need to track utilities, repairs, or other expenses related to your home.

There are two limitations to keep in mind:

1. The deduction is limited to 300 square feet (a $1,500 deduction)
2. No deduction is allowed if you have a loss on your Schedule C

Example 1 - Julie has a 10 x 10 (100 square foot) home office, which she uses exclusively in her photography business. She has a net profit on her Schedule C for the tax year. She would be allowed a $500 deduction on her Schedule C to offset her business income. (100 square feet x $5/foot = $500 deduction)

Example 2 - Thomas has a storage shed he uses solely to store inventory for his online sales business. It is a 20 x 20 (400 square foot) space. The calculated deduction would be $2,000 (400 square foot x $5/foot = $2,000). However, the simplified method is limited, so Thomas's home office deduction on his Schedule C would be capped at $1,500 for the tax year.

Regular Method (Long Calculation)

If you keep good books and records, and don't mind gathering receipts at tax time, you may be able to take a larger deduction by calculating your deduction via the regular method. In the regular method, you take any expenses related to the operation of your home and prorate those by the square footage of your home office to your total home square footage.

There are some common expenses to track in calculating the deduction via this method:

- Real estate tax
- Mortgage interest -or- Rent
- Electric bills
- Heating bills
- Repairs on your home and/or office space
- Depreciation of the home

EXAMPLE

Example 3 - Andrew has significant real estate taxes and mortgage interest, so he has found that utilizing the regular method results in a larger tax deduction. He has a 10 x 12 home office in a 2,800 square foot home.

His 120 square foot office is 4.3% of his home (120/2,800). Therefore, he can choose to take the simplified deduction, which would be $600 ($120 x $5) or the regular method, which is $653 for the year.

Electric	$1,200
Heat	1,500
Real Estate Taxes	4,300
Mortgage Interest	7,250
Repairs	945
Total Expenses	$15,195
x proration rate	x .043
Regular Method	**$653**

S-Corporations and Employees Not Eligible

This deduction is another one of those cases where keeping things simple in your business sometimes pays off. This deduction is only available to sole proprietors (or SMLLCs) or partners in partnerships. S-corporations are not eligible for this deduction. If shareholders are utilizing a home office, they should create a written agreement with the corporation and be reimbursed monthly for the use of their home office, just as they would be for any other business-related expenses.

Employees have not been eligible for this deduction since the TCJA tax law changes in 2017. But to be honest, most didn't receive a benefit after calculating the deduction, as it was an itemized deduction and limited on the Schedule A. This was one area of the tax code that didn't ultimately benefit a large portion of taxpayers, so Congress agreed on removing the deduction for unreimbursed employee expenses.

If you are using a home office as a remote worker, you have a couple of options. You can quietly thank your lucky stars they haven't forced you back to the office, or you can try to negotiate a reimbursement to offset some of your overhead expenses (like internet and electric bills) as part of your salary package.

Regular Calculation

A) Square footage of home (total usable space)

_____

B) Square footage of space used exclusively for business

_____

C) Simplified deduction allowed (B * $5) maximum of 300 square feet ($1,500 deduction) allowed for simplified method

_____

D) Percentage to use for indirect expenses (B / A)

_____

E) Date home purchased

_____

F) Date started using home office

_____

G) Cost of home when purchased

_____

H) Value of land when purchased home

_____

I) Cost of improvements made to home since purchase

_____

J) Current fair market value (FMV) of home

_____

Items E through J will be used to calculate the depreciation expense on the home in the regular calculation.

Expense	Indirect (Entire Home)	Direct (Only for Office)
Mortgage Interest	$_____	$_____
Real Estate Taxes	$_____	$_____
Minor Repairs	$_____	$_____
Major Repairs	$_____	$_____
Electric	$_____	$_____
Gas	$_____	$_____
Rent	$_____	$_____
_____	$_____	$_____
_____	$_____	$_____
_____	$_____	$_____
Total Expenses	$_____	$_____
	Prorate these expenses for home office	*Take 100% of these for home office*

Indirect expenses are those related to the whole home that need to be prorated, such as your electric bill, mortgage interest, repairs to the roof of the home, etc.

Direct expenses are those related directly to the home office itself. These would include items such as replacing carpet in that room, an electric bill if it's billed separately from the rest of the home, etc.

Home Office Deduction
Can You Deduct Business Use of the Home Expenses?

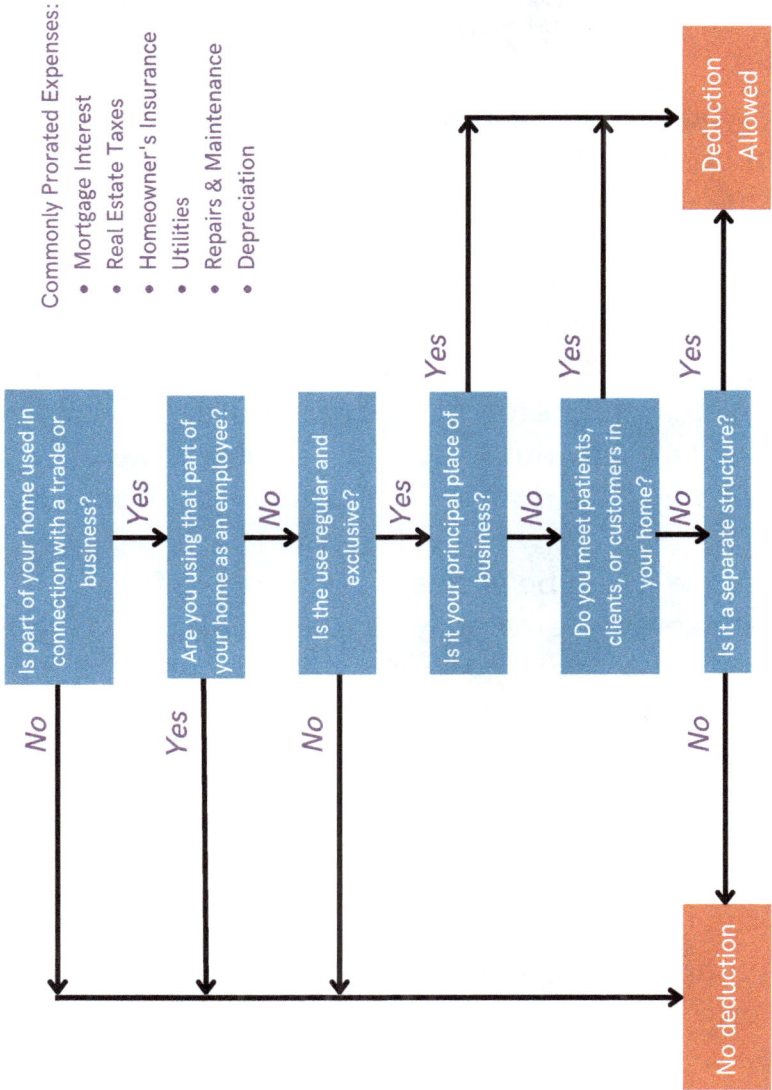

Commonly Prorated Expenses:
- Mortgage Interest
- Real Estate Taxes
- Homeowner's Insurance
- Utilities
- Repairs & Maintenance
- Depreciation

Is part of your home used in connection with a trade or business?
— No → No deduction
— Yes →

Are you using that part of your home as an employee?
— Yes → No deduction
— No →

Is the use regular and exclusive?
— No → No deduction
— Yes →

Is it your principal place of business?
— Yes → Deduction Allowed
— No →

Do you meet patients, clients, or customers in your home?
— Yes → Deduction Allowed
— No →

Is it a separate structure?
— Yes → Deduction Allowed
— No → No deduction

Chapter Twelve

Hiring Your Child - Big Tax & Retirement Savings

If you are a sole proprietor and haven't yet hired your child in your business, you may be missing out on a massive tax saving opportunity. This is available only to sole proprietors (and single-member LLCs), so this is one time when simpler is better in your business. If you are unaware of the benefits of hiring your children, or just haven't given it much thought as you've grown, take careful note of this chapter. There are some great tidbits that could save you money now and set your child up for a massive retirement nest-egg later.

I know it can be almost impossible to find extra cash to pay someone when you are building a business. You may be wondering how to pay yourself each week, let alone putting anyone else, including your child, on payroll. But what if you just got creative in this area? This is one place that it may help to think outside the box and teach your child the value of money at the same time.

What if your child started performing age-appropriate tasks in the business and then paid for their own soccer camps, dance lessons, or kayak they've been eyeing with their weekly paycheck? And what if you saved taxes at the same time?

There are some basic rules to follow so you're not running afoul of the IRS or child labor laws. It's great to think outside the box, but let's not get so creative that we find ourselves in trouble with any 3-letter agencies. Here are things to keep in mind as you draft your plan and before you warn your child that work starts at 9 am sharp on Monday morning.

Business Eligibility

As I noted earlier, this tax savings benefit is available only to sole proprietors. Yep, this is a benefit aimed directly at small business owners! And yes, this includes those registered as LLCs, as long as you are a single-member LLC, and have not elected to be taxed as an S-Corporation.

Qualified Joint Venture Exception

There is a qualified joint venture exception, If the only partners in a business are spouses and you are the parents of the child being hired. You must both materially participate in the business and elect to be taxed as a qualified joint venture (QJV). A QJV election requires that the husband and wife file 2 Schedule C's for their share of income, rather than a partnership return.

This is an IRS election on your tax return, so be sure to discuss this situation with a CPA or tax advisor to ensure the proper elections are filed before putting your child on payroll. It can be costly to repay self-employment or other taxes if your i's aren't dotted and your t's aren't crossed with the IRS.

Legitimate Employees

When you put your children on payroll, be sure to treat them as you would any other employee from a financial and legal standpoint. The more documentation you have and the more structured arrangement you create, the better off you are in showing that your child is truly an employee earning a paycheck, even if they are only 7 years old and filing papers for you.

✓ **Performing Legitimate Work** - Your child must perform real, age-appropriate, work in your business.

✓ **Receiving Reasonable Pay** - The child's pay must match what you would pay an unrelated party with the same skill set to perform the tasks. Would you pay someone else $50/hour to shred papers for you? If the answer is "no", then your child may need to be content with their $10/hour paycheck.

✓ **Focusing on Record-Keeping** - Track your child's hours, tasks, and payments, just as you would any other employee. Keep those records handy, should the IRS or DOL ask for them.

✓ **Following Child Labor Laws** - There is no federal age minimum when hiring children in sole proprietorships, but state child labor laws may restrict their hours and responsibilities. Keep your child's hours reasonable and within age restrictions in your state.

Tax Savings Opportunities

The tax savings opportunities are multi-layered for you and for your child. It starts with federal and self-employment tax savings for you , flows through to zero (or low) federal taxes for your child, and can culminate with non-taxable retirement for your child, if you take advantage of available IRA contributions opportunities. As with all tax regulations, the devil is in the details, so follow the steps in this chapter carefully, watch age limits carefully, and make sure your payroll system is set up properly.

✓ **Business Deduction** - The child's wages are deductible in the business just as any other employee wages would be. This saves you federal and self-employment taxes.

✓ **FICA Tax Savings** - Children under 18 are exempt from FICA taxes (Social Security & Medicare) on wages paid by their parent's business. Not only have you saved on your own self-employment taxes, but your business doesn't have to pay FICA on behalf of your child and your child doesn't have to have it withheld from their wages either. Win/win/win!

✓ **FUTA Tax Savings** - Children under 21 are exempt from federal unemployment (FUTA) taxes, which saves the business money each payroll.

✓ **Zero Federal Taxes for Child** - If the wages are under the standard deduction ($14,000 in 2025) the child will pay no federal tax.

✓ **IRA Contributions & Tax-Free Retirement** - Since wages are earned income, you can make IRA contributions on behalf of the child. The 2025 contribution limit is $7,000, or their earned income, whichever is less.

✓ **BONUS** - If you make Roth IRA contributions, those distributions (including any earnings) are tax-free when your child retires.

NOTE: A federal tax return isn't typically required if the only income is W2 earnings below the standard deduction. But any earnings above the standard deduction would trigger the need for a federal tax return to be filed and potential taxes to be paid on behalf of the child. There may also be state and/or local tax filings triggered by the child's wages.

Proper tax planning will result in the biggest tax savings benefit all around.

Have you considered hiring your adorable toddler to create social media ads? This could be a great way to put some money into an IRA for your child. Just document everything, and be sure to stay on the right side of your state's labor laws.

Gusto Sign-up Bonus:

Need a payroll provider? For a limited time, Gusto will give you a $100 Visa gift card once you run your first payroll. Follow the QR code below for a link to current bonuses.

EXAMPLE

You pay your 12-year-old $8,500 in 2025 for performing administrative tasks in your office.

- You can deduct the $8,500 in wages on your business tax return, saving you both federal & self-employment taxes.
- If your child has no other income, a federal return filing will not be required and your child will owe no federal taxes, as the wages are below the current standard deduction of $14,000.
- Your child will not have to have FICA taxes withheld from their wages, and the business will not have to pay matching FICA taxes, as the child is under 18 years old.
- Your business will not have to pay federal unemployment (FUTA) taxes on the child's wages as they are under 21 years old.
- Your child can contribute $7,000 to an IRA. If the $7,000 is contributed to a Roth IRA, they can withdraw both contributions and earnings at retirement tax-free.
- Place the child's wages into their own bank account to show the IRS and DOL that the child was, in fact, paid for the time worked.
- Pay for activities or other needs of the child from their earnings, but keep good records. All earnings should be able to be traced to receipts for the expenditures to avoid any hint of improperly using funds that legally belong to the child. (You've effectively paid for dance lessons with tax-free money. 🎉)

At a Glance

☐ Confirm your business is structured as a sole proprietorship, single-member LLC, or qualified joint venture

☐ Hire your child to perform services for your business

☐ Track your child's hours and duties performed in the business

☐ Pay your child via payroll (consider using a payroll service for payroll processing and tax filings)

☐ If your child is under 18, confirm no FICA taxes are withheld or paid by you on their wages

☐ If your child is under 21, forego paying federal unemployment taxes on their wages

☐ File quarterly payroll returns and W2s to ensure the IRS sees these as legitimate wages

☐ Deduct the wages on your Schedule C, just as you would with wages paid to other employees

☐ If your child's only income is wages that fall below the standard deduction ($14,000 in 2025), no federal tax filing is required

☐ Consider putting money into a traditional or Roth IRA for your child (up to $7,000 or their wages, whichever is lower)

Chapter Thirteen

Hiring Employees - Understanding the True Cost

There may come a time in your business when you feel ready to hire your first employee. You've been wearing all the hats for too long. And maybe you've hired some subcontractors along the way, but now you need another set of hands in-house to assist with day-to-day tasks.

Onboarding your first employee can be daunting. How much will you pay them and how often? What tax numbers do you need? What are your state laws with regard to minimum wage, hours, and benefits? What is the best system to use to run payroll? There is a long list of questions to answer. However, once you have processes in place, the employee can prove to be a game-changer in your business.

This chapter will walk you through the thought process you should complete before setting out to hire your first employee, the true costs of adding employees to your business, and a checklist to follow to ensure you won't miss any important tasks along the way.

Making the Decision

Before you draft the job posting, consider the time it will take to hire, train, and manage an employee. Are you ready and willing to add Human Resource manager to your list of job titles? An employee can free up time for you to tackle other tasks, but you will also need to set aside time to train and manage them as they grow with your business.

Use this section to gather your thoughts and ideas on fitting this new person into your business. Take some time to answer some of the following questions to ensure you're ready for a new person to join your team:

What tasks will they perform?

_____

_____

_____

_____

_____

What qualifications should they possess?

_____

_____

_____

_____

_____

How many hours per week will the employee be needed?

_____

_____

_____

_____

_____

Is this a seasonal/temporary position, or will it be permanent?

_____

_____

_____

_____

_____

Do you understand your state laws regarding minimum wage, time off requirements, employee benefits, etc? (Consider hiring a professional human resource company to guide you.)

_____

_____

_____

_____

_____

Costs of Hiring

Many small business owners factor in the hourly rate when budgeting for an employee, only to be shocked by the true cost on a weekly basis. Where did all of the payroll tax and insurance costs come from? It can quickly derail a small business on a tight budget.

Keep in mind that a new employee will be counting on the agreed-upon hours and weekly pay to cover their bills. Review your budget carefully to ensure you can still pay yourself before taking on this additional financial responsibility. As tough as it is to hire your first employee, it's much harder to let that employee go if you find that you can no longer afford their services.

Common Employee Costs

Below is a list of common costs associated with hiring an employee. Take each of these into account when completing your budget and calculating the true effect of the employee on your cash flows.

Wages, Taxes & Benefits

- Hourly wage
- Social Security tax 6.2% (up to $176,100 in wages for 2025)
- Medicare tax 1.45%
- Federal unemployment tax .6% (up to $7,000 in wages for 2025)
- State unemployment tax (rates & wage limits vary by state)

- Workers' compensation insurance (rates vary by state and type of business)
- Health insurance
- IRA or 401(k) contributions
- Payroll processing fees

Other Common Employee Costs

- Employee licenses & dues
- Tools & equipment (such as computers & office supplies)
- Software subscriptions
- Creation of employee policy manual
- Office or work space for the employee

Calculation

Gross Wages		Calculate Gross Wages
Hourly Rate		$_____
Average Weekly Hours	X	$_____
Weekly Wages	=	$_____
	-OR-	
Annual Salary		$_____
Weekly Salary (Salary/52)		$_____

Payroll Taxes & Benefits		Calculate on Hourly/Salary Pay
Social Security (Employee)	6.2% (.062)	$_____
Social Security (Employer)	6.2% (.062)	$_____
Medicare (Employee)	1.45% (.0145)	$_____
Medicare (Employer)	1.45% (.0145)	$_____
Federal Unemployment	.06% (.0006)	$_____
State Unemployment	_____%	$_____
Workers' Comp Insurance	$_____/pay	$_____
Health Insurance	$_____/pay	$_____
Pension Contribution	_____%/pay	$_____
Payroll Processing Fee	$_____/pay	$_____
Total Anticipated Weekly Gross Wages Plus Taxes/Benefits		$_____

Paying Payroll Taxes

Submitting payroll taxes timely is imperative. More than one small business has come to me in a panic because they were behind in taxes and at risk of losing their business. The IRS treats payroll tax liabilities differently from other taxes due to them and the penalties for late payment are more severe with fewer options for forgiveness.

The IRS refers to the employee's withheld taxes as "trust fund" liabilities. This is because the employer is temporarily holding the employee's money in trust until it is handed over to the IRS. If you fail to remit the employee's withholdings, you are not only withholding money from the IRS, but stealing from the employee in the IRS eyes. The IRS will pursue these taxes and related penalties with a vengeance and the liabilities will not go away, even in the case of bankruptcies.

Some payroll taxes have to be paid weekly, while others need to be paid monthly or quarterly. To be on the safe side, and to ensure all payments are made timely, consider using a third-party payroll processor that will make these payments for you. They typically withdraw the employee's wages and any related taxes each payday. The payroll processor then bears the responsibility of submitting those payments to the proper agencies and filing any required quarterly and annual reports.

Taking advantage of an online payroll processor will allow you to process payroll in a matter of minutes so you can get back to running your business.

Payroll Setup Checklist

- [ ] Confirm your comfort level with managing people
- [ ] Create job description
- [ ] Create job qualifications
- [ ] Research average pay ranges in your area
- [ ] Research state employment laws
- [ ] Apply for an Employer Identification Number
- [ ] Apply for a state tax withholding account number
- [ ] Apply for an unemployment tax account number
- [ ] Apply for workers' compensation insurance
- [ ] Choose your third-party payroll processing company
- [ ] Create an employee manual
- [ ] Purchase a labor law poster
- [ ] Purchase a computer & other supplies for employee
- [ ] Pre-screen potential employees for Work Opportunity Tax Credit

Slow walk your hiring process. Taking the time to hire the right individual at the right time can save you time, money, and frustration in the long run.

Employee Onboarding Checklist

- [ ] Prepare offer letter
- [ ] Set up workstation
- [ ] Prepare onboarding materials (employee handbook, benefits info, etc)
- [ ] Create employee accounts (email, payroll, access to company systems)
- [ ] Enroll employee in payroll system
- [ ] Have employee complete W-4 for federal withholding on W2
- [ ] Have employee complete state tax withholding form
- [ ] Have employee complete I-9
  Have employee complete direct deposit form
- [ ] Enroll employee in workers' compensation insurance
- [ ] Complete Work Opportunity Tax Credit paperwork, if employee eligible
- [ ] Discuss company benefits with employee
- [ ] Have employee complete benefits paperwork (health insurance, 401k, etc)
- [ ] Have employee acknowledge confidentiality or non-compete agreements
- [ ] Enroll employee in any necessary training
- [ ] Copy employee's required licenses/certifications

Employee or Subcontractor?

One area that is receiving increased scrutiny is the misclassification of employees as subcontractors. A business owner should take care in properly classifying a worker. Are they an employee, and eligible for the protections and benefits that go along with that classification? Or are they subcontractors and responsible for their own tax payments and related filings?

Reporting Differences

Companies often decide to treat workers as subcontractors to avoid the burden of running payroll, especially if they are small and only have one employee. Subcontractors receive a 1099 at year end and are responsible for submitting quarterly payroll estimates to cover any taxes due on income earned. This also means they are paying both the employee and the employer halves of FICA tax, and they are probably not covered by the employer's unemployment or workers' compensation insurance policies.

An employee should receive a W-2 at year end and the employer is responsible for withholding and remitting all payroll taxes on their behalf. They are also covered by minimum wage, overtime pay, and other employee benefit regulations.

If an employer misclassifies an employee as a subcontractor, there are consequences. If the IRS deems that a worker was indeed an employee, they can recalculate prior payroll tax returns to determine the amount of payroll taxes that should have been paid in on behalf of the employee. The employer will be responsible for paying these taxes, plus penalties and interest, regardless of whether or not the individual had paid in the taxes as a subcontractor. The Department of Labor may also sanction the employer for missed overtime or other benefits as required by various state laws.

Below are categories the IRS has provided to help decide on the proper classification:

Behavioral Control

Does the business have the right to direct and control the work performed? Review the following categories:

- Type of instructions given; such as when & where to work and what tools or services to use or purchase
- Degree of instructions given; the more detailed the instructions, the more likely the individual is to be classified as an employee
- Evaluation systems implemented & a high level of job training given may point to an employee

Financial Control

Does the business have the right to control the financial aspects of the job?

- Who bears the responsibility for investments in the equipment and other expenses related to the job?

- Is there opportunity for profit or loss on the job for the worker?
- Is the worker free to market the same skills elsewhere and to set the price for the job being performed?

Relationship

Written contracts will help establish the classification, although a contract stating someone is a subcontractor is not in and of itself enough. You should also review:

- Is the individual eligible for vacation pay or a pension plan?
- How permanent is the relationship? Is it for a fixed term from the outset?
- Are the services performed key to business operations?

Employee Gifts

Reporting of employee gifts is an area that is often mishandled by employers and can lead to loss of business deductions and payment of back payroll taxes plus penalties and interest if the IRS should review your books. I can empathize with employers who want to give employees gifts at Christmas or other important times without putting them on the W-2. It doesn't seem fair to tax employees on something the employer is trying to do to reward an employee. However, Congress has created very clear laws on the reporting of employee gifts and they have a very Grinchy feeling to them.

Most gifts given to employees are taxable items and must be included in income (the W-2) at year end, unless accounting for it would be an administrative burden. Items that must be included in an employee's wages include:

- Cash (regardless of amount)
- Gift Cards (regardless of amount)
- Tangible personal items (unless minimal in value)

There are a few items which are allowed to be excluded from income per the current tax code:

- Gift cards for specific merchandise (of minimal value - such as a turkey)
- Occasional flowers or fruit
- Occasional theater or sporting tickets
- Group parties or picnics

If you would like to make sure that an employee receives a specific amount (such as a $500 holiday bonus), you can "gross up" the figure in your payroll system to ensure the employee receives the intended amount, but all taxes are paid properly. In this instance, the employer is paying both halves of the FICA taxes. So, the final gross payroll figure for that employee would be more than the $500 gift, but it does keep the employer on the right side of the IRS.

Appendix

Glossary - From Unfamiliar to Empowering

Many small business owners shy away from having important discussions with their accountant, banker, or attorney because of complicated and unfamiliar terminology. I hope that this sections helps you understand the terminology a bit better. remove some of the overwhelm, and encourages you to become more educated and empowered in your business. If you are working with a professional that isn't willing to answer questions, or one that makes you feel uneducated without taking time to educate you, I encourage you to interview some additional professionals until you find one that makes you feel comfortable and in control of your business and finances.

Term	Definition	Example
1099 Form	A form you send to freelancers or contractors you paid for services (or rent), telling the government about the money you gave them so they can properly report for tax purposes.	A web developer pays a freelance coder $8,000 and files a 1099-NEC form with the IRS by January 31 to report it.

Term	Definition	Example
Accounts Payable	Money you owe suppliers for goods or services you got on credit.	A caterer buys $1,000 in ingredients on 30-day terms and records it as accounts payable until payment is made.
Accounts Receivable	Money customers owe you for products or services you've already delivered.	A plumber finishes a $2,500 job and invoices the client, adding $2,500 to accounts receivable until the invoice is paid.
Accrual Basis Accounting	Recording income when you earn it (accounts receivable) and expenses when you owe them (accounts payable), even if cash hasn't changed hands yet.	A marketing firm records $5,000 in revenue when they complete a campaign and invoice the client, even if the client pays 60 days later.
Amortization	Spreading out the cost of intangible assets (like patents or software) over time for tax deductions, similar to depreciation but for non-physical items.	A software developer buys a $10,000 patent and amortizes $2,000 per year over five years as a tax deduction on their return.

Term	Definition	Example
Assets	Things your business owns that have value, such as cash, equipment, or inventory you can sell.	A landscaping company lists their truck ($15,000), tools ($5,000), and $3,000 in cash as assets on their balance sheet.
Balance Sheet	A snapshot report of what your business owns (assets), owes (debts), and the owner's share (equity) at a specific moment in time.	A small bakery at the end of the month lists $15,000 in cash and equipment (assets), $8,000 in supplier bills (liabilities), and the net balance of $7,000 as owner equity.
Break-even Analysis	A calculation to figure out how much you need to sell to cover all your costs with no income or loss at the end of the period.	A shoe store with $10,000 monthly fixed costs and $50 variable cost per $200 shoe needs to sell 67 pairs to break even ($10,000 /(200 - 50)).

Term	Definition	Example
Budget	A plan that estimates how much money you'll earn and spend over a set time, helping you to avoid overspending.	A boutique owner creates a yearly budget projecting $120,000 in sales and allocating $40,000 for inventory, $20,000 for rent, and $10,000 for marketing. They monitor this monthly to ensure they meet sales and net income goals.
Business Loan	Money you borrow from a bank or lender to grow your business, which you pay back with interest.	A food truck owner borrows $25,000 from a bank to buy a new truck and repays $500 monthly over five years.
Capital Gain	The profit you make when selling an asset (such as stock) for more than you paid, which may be taxed at a special rate.	An employee bought company stock @ $10/share. They sell the stock when they leave the company for $25/share. They pay tax on the $15 difference at a capital-gains tax rate, which is lower than the ordinary rate they pay on their salary.

Term	Definition	Example
Cash Basis Accounting	A simple way to track money where you record income when cash comes in and expenses when it goes out.	A handyman records $1,000 income only when the client pays the invoice, not when the job is done.
Cash Flow	The actual money coming in and going out of your business over time, often done by tracking your checking account balance.	A bookstore receives $8,000 from book sales but pays $6,000 for rent and inventory, resulting in a $2,000 positive cash flow for the month.
Cost of Goods Sold (COGS)	The direct costs of making or buying the products you sell, such as materials and labor.	A candle maker spends $1,750 on wax, $200 on wicks, and $450 on jars for a total of $2,400 in cost of goods to produce candles they will sell in their store.
Depreciation	Spreading out the cost of big purchases (like a building) over years for tax purposes, instead of deducting it all at once.	An attorney buys a $450,000 building and depreciates $11,538 per year over 39 years on their taxes.

Term	Definition	Example
Effective Tax Rate	The real percentage of your business's total income that ends up going to taxes, after figuring in all deductions and credits.	If your consulting firm reports $100,000 in taxable income and owes $20,000 in federal taxes after deductions, your effective tax rate is 20%.
EIN (Employer Identification Number)	A unique nine-digit number the government gives your business, like an individual's Social Security number, but for tax and hiring purposes.	When starting a freelance writing business, you apply for an EIN on the IRS website to open a business bank account and hire your first part-time editor.
Employee	A person you hire full- or part-time, pay wages or salary, and control how they do their job, when they work, and how much they are paid.	A coffee shop hires a barista for 40 hours a week at $15/hour. The coffee shop controls their hours, pays some taxes on the employee's behalf, and offers some benefits.
Equity	The value left in your business after subtracting your liabilities (what you owe) from your assets (what you own).	A sole proprietor has $50,000 in assets (cash and equipment) and $20,000 in liabilities (accounts payable and bank loans). Their equity is $30,000.

Term	Definition	Example
Estimated Taxes	Regular payments you send to the government throughout the year for taxes on your business profits, so you don't owe a big lump sum at at year-end.	A graphic designer earning $60,000 annually pays $1,500 each quarter to the IRS to cover federal and self-employment taxes on their freelance income.
Expenses	Everyday costs your business pays, like office supplies or advertising, which help you business stay open and which you can often subtract from income to save on taxes.	An online store has $500 in website hosting fees, $150 in telephone & internet, and $200 in business meals related to the business. Some of these may not be deductible, but they all help the owner run and grow the business.
Fair Market Value	The price an item or asset would sell for in an open market between willing buyers and sellers.	A used delivery van for a catering business is appraised at $12,000 fair market value when listing it for sale.

Term	Definition	Example
Fixed Costs	Expenses that stay the same each month, no matter how much you sell, such as rent or insurance.	A yoga studio pays $1,200 monthly rent and $300 for insurance, totaling $1,500 in fixed costs. These are due each month, regardless of class attendance.
Grant	Free money from the government or organizations to start or grow your business. These funds do not have to be paid back.	A tech startup receives a $10,000 SBA grant for women-owned businesses to develop an app prototype. This may be taxable income, but is not a loan and does not have to be repaid.
Gross Margin	Your sales minus the cost of goods sold. This tells you the profit before other expenses such as rent, insurance, & office supplies.	A bakery sells $20,000 in cakes with $12,000 COGS, leaving an $8,000 gross margin or 40%.
Home Office Deduction	A way to reduce your taxes by claiming part of your home expenses (such as rent or utilities) when you use a space exclusively to run your business.	A consultant using 200 sq ft of their 1,000 sq ft apartment to manage their business deducts 20% of their $1,200 monthly rent, or $240, on their Schedule C.

Glossary

Term	Definition	Example
Liabilities	Money your business owes to others, such as loans or unpaid bills (accounts payable).	A boutique owes $4,000 on a credit card for inventory and $10,000 on a small business loan, for a total of $14,000 in liabilities.
Line of Credit	A flexible loan from a bank where you can borrow up to a set amount as needed, paying interest only on what you use, much like a business credit card.	A retail store has a $20,000 line of credit and draws $5,000 to cover seasonal inventory. The store can pay interest only on the loan until sales are sufficient to pay back the principal.
Liquidity	How quickly your business can turn assets into cash to pay bills without losing much value.	A consultant with $20,000 in cash and easy-to-collect invoices has high liquidity to cover a sudden $5,000 equipment repair.
LLC (Limited Liability Company)	A flexible business setup that is incorporated within a state of your choosing and protects your personal assets from business debts.	A landlord creates an LLC when they purchase a rental property to protect their personal assets should a tenant slip and fall on ice during the winter.

Term	Definition	Example
Mileage Deduction	A tax break for using your car for business purposes. It is calculated by multiplying miles driven for business by a standard rate set by the government.	A real estate agent drives 10,000 business miles in a year and deducts $7,000 using the 2025 IRS rate of 70 cents per mile.
Net Income	The actual profit left after subtracting all expenses from your total revenue. Often referred to as the "bottom line".	A pet grooming service has $50,000 in revenue minus $35,000 in expenses (supplies, rent, and wages), leaving $15,000 in net income for the quarter.
Non-Deductible Expenses	Costs your business pays that you can't subtract from income to reduce taxes, such as fines, penalties, or half of any business meals.	A parking ticket you receive while taking products to the post office for your online store can't be deducted, even though it happened while running a business errand.
Owner Contribution	Cash or assets you, as the owner, put into the business from your personal funds to start it up or help it grow. These contributions are not treated as income.	You transfer $10,000 from your personal savings into the business account to buy a new computer for your freelance graphic design work.

Term	Definition	Example
Owner Distribution	Money you, as the business owner, take out of the business profits for personal use. These withdrawals don't count as a business expense.	If your coffee shop earns $50,000 in profit after expenses, you might distribute $2,000 monthly in cash to yourself for living expenses.
Pass-Through Entity	A business type (such as a partnership or S-Corporation) where profits "pass through" to an owner's personal tax return based on their ownership percentage.	A yoga studio earns $60,000 in profit. The two partners each own 50% of the studio and pay tax at their individual rates on $30,000 of income for the year.
Payroll Taxes	Mandatory federal, state, and local taxes that employers and employees pay on salaries and wages.	An florist uses a payroll system to ensure federal withholding, Social Security, Medicare, unemployment and state & local taxes are withheld and remitted from their employee's paycheck to avoid penalties & interest.

Term	Definition	Example
Profit and Loss Statement (Income Statement)	A summary of your business's sales, costs of good sold, and expenses over a period (such as a month or year) to show if you made a profit or loss.	A freelance graphic designer's monthly P&L shows $10,000 in client fees (revenue), and $3,000 in expenses (software, advertising, and subscriptions), resulting in a $7,000 net profit.
Profit Margin	This is the profit remaining after deducting the Cost of Goods Sold (COGS) from revenue. It shows how efficiently a company produces its goods or services.	A handmade jewelry seller has $10,000 in sales and $6,000 in materials & shipping costs, giving a 40% profit margin ($4,000 profit / $10,000 sales).
ROI (Return on Investment)	A way to measure if your spending on a specific expense made more money than it cost.	Spending $1,000 on Facebook ads brings $3,000 in new sales, yielding a 200% ROI (($3,000 - $1,000) / $1,000 x 100).

Term	Definition	Example
S-Corporation	A business structure similar to a regular corporation but with pass-through taxes (profits taxed on owners' personal returns) and limited to 100 shareholders.	A family-owned auto repair shop elects S-Corp status, so $80,000 in profits passes to the three owners' personal taxes without incurring corporate tax.
Self-Employment Tax	Taxes you pay into the Social Security & Medicare systems if you're your own boss. You pay both the employee and employer portions.	A freelance photographer earning $40,000 pays 15.3% in self-employment tax, or about $6,120, along with their federal taxes at the end of the year.
Sole Proprietorship	The simplest business setup where you and the business are the same person for taxes and liability.	A neighborhood dog walker operates as a sole proprietorship, reporting all income on their personal tax return.
Subcontractor	An independent worker or company you hire for a specific job or part of a project. They handle their own taxes and aren't your employee.	A construction firm hires a plumber as a subcontractor for a one-week job on a renovation, paying them $2,500 without withholding taxes.

Term	Definition	Example
Tax Credit	A direct dollar-for-dollar cut in the taxes your business owes. It lowers your tax bill more powerfully than a deduction.	Hiring a full-time veteran qualifies your bakery for the Work Opportunity Tax Credit, reducing your tax bill by up to $2,400 for that employee.
Tax Deductions	Expenses you subtract from your business income to lower the amount you ultimately pay taxes on.	A coffee shop owner deducts $5,000 spent on coffee beans and cups from their sales income, reducing their taxable income on their Form 1040.
Term Loan	A lump-sum loan where you get the proceeds upfront. The loan is paid back in fixed monthly payments over a set period of time.	A tech startup borrows $50,000 as a term loan to buy computers and office equipment, repaying $1,000 monthly over five years, including interest & principal.
Variable Costs	Costs that change based on how much you produce or sell, such as materials for products.	A t-shirt printing business spends $5 per shirt on ink and fabric. These costs would change as the prices of t-shirts or ink fluctuate.

Term	Definition	Example
W-2 Form	A form the government requires you to give employees at year-end, showing how much they earned and how much in taxes were withheld.	A retail shop owner sends a W-2 to their cashier showing $25,000 in wages and $3,000 in federal taxes that were withheld.
Working Capital	The cash left over after paying short-term bills. This shows if your business has enough money to run day-to-day.	A food truck has $25,000 in cash minus $15,000 in bills due soon, leaving $10,000 in working capital.

Appendix

Important Business Information

Legal Business Name
_____

Incorporation Date
_____

State of Incorporation
_____

Entity Type
_____

EIN
_____

Physical Address
_____

Mailing Address
_____

Phone Number
_____

Domain Provider
_____

Domain Name
_____

Website Address
_____

E-Mail Provider
_____

E-Mail Address

_____

Facebook Handle

_____

Instagram Handle

_____

X Handle

_____

TikTok Handle

_____

Accountant

_____

Attorney

_____

Insurance Agent

_____

_____

_____

_____

_____

Notes

Notes

Notes

Notes

www.ingramcontent.com/pod-product-compliance
Lightning Source LLC
Chambersburg PA
CBHW060537210326
41519CB00014B/3252